DAY HIKES ON
MAUI

55 GREAT HIKES

by Robert Stone

Day Hike Books, Inc.
RED LODGE, MONTANA

Published by Day Hike Books, Inc.
P.O. Box 865
Red Lodge, Montana 59068

Distributed by The Globe Pequot Press
246 Goose Lane
P.O. Box 480
Guilford, CT 06437-0480
800-243-0495 (direct order) · 800-820-2329 (fax order)
www.globe-pequot.com

Photographs by Robert Stone
Design by Paula Doherty

The author has made every attempt to provide accurate information
in this book. However, trail routes and features may change please
use common sense and forethought, and be mindful of your own
capabilities. Let this book guide you, but be aware that each hiker
assumes responsibility for their own safety. The author and publisher
do not assume any responsibility for loss, damage or injury caused
through the use of this book.

Cover photo: Iao Needle, Hikes 13 and 14.
Back cover photo: Waianapanapa State Park, Hikes 47 and 48.

Table of Contents

Southwest Coast
Kihea, Wailea and Makena

North Coast
Kahului to Paia

The Upcountry
PoliPoli State Park

The Upcountry
Haleakala National Park

North and East Coast
The Hana Highway

About the Hikes

Many of Maui's most beautiful and unique attractions are easily accessible by foot. *Day Hikes on Maui* takes you to 55 of the island's best hikes, including the entire coastline and the upcountry regions of West Maui and Haleakala National Park. All levels of hiking experience are accommodated in this guide, with an emphasis on outstanding scenery and memorable features. Each hike includes a map, detailed driving and hiking directions and a summary. An overall map of Maui and the locations of the hikes is found on the next page.

Geographically, Maui is surprisingly diverse. Within an hour you may go from verdant, humid rain forests to the stark, cold and fascinating lunar landscape of the Haleakala crater. Hikes range from gentle beach strolls along the undulating coastline to steep mountain trails with sweeping views of the entire island. To help you decide which hikes are most appealing to you, a brief summary of the highlights is included with each hike. You may enjoy these areas for a short time or the whole day. The hikes in this guide are roughly divided into coastal hikes, the upcountry, and the Hana Highway.

Visions of Hawaii often include temperate sandy beaches, crystal-clear tidepools, secluded coves, and the surf crashing into a jagged lava coastline. You will find just such a landscape along the coastal hikes in West Maui and the island's southwest perimeter. Explore world-class beaches, sea caves, turquoise ocean bays, lava flows, dormant cones, ancient Hawaiian sites and steep canyons with waterfalls. Traveling just a few miles inland takes you to West Maui's emerald green interior, including the mossy mantle of the Iao Needle (cover photo).

On the island's east lobe, the upcountry region includes Polipoli State Park in a quiet, meditative forest with an understory of ferns and mosses. Extensive trails cross through this forest reserve on the west slopes of Haleakala and connect with the volcano's summit.

To the west of this state park is Haleakala National Park, extending from the 10,023-foot summit of Maui to the coastline. The unique park is embraces the world's largest dormant volcano—Haleakala. Several hikes explore this magnificent area, from the crater rim to the barren landscape of the crater floor.

One of the most scenic drives in all Hawaii is along the Hana Highway. This gorgeous, winding 55-mile road traverses the northeast slopes of Haleakala along the edge of the windward coastal cliffs. Hikes found along this road include waterfalls, freshwater swimming pools, deep canyons, seascape vistas, over 600 curves and more than fifty one-lane bridges. After visiting the charming town of Hana, the road continues to Oheo Gulch, where the flows of Haleakala once spilled into the ocean. A series of descending pools cascade into each other through this gulch before emerging with the Pacific out of a rock grotto.

The thought of exploring Maui may cause you to don tank tops and sandals. Winds, high elevations, wet rain forests and dry deserts will make it necessary to have a variety of clothing when exploring Maui. Bring hats (for both hot and cool weather), jackets and gloves. Sunscreen, insect repellent, sunglasses, drinking water and snacks are a must. Elevations are as high as 10,000 feet and surprisingly chilly. You will very likely need warm clothing when exploring the peaks and valleys of Haleakala. But also be sure to bring swimwear and outdoor gear to enjoy the coastal areas for the day.

Your time on Maui will be enhanced by exploring Maui's unique geography. Enjoy the trails and incredible scenery!

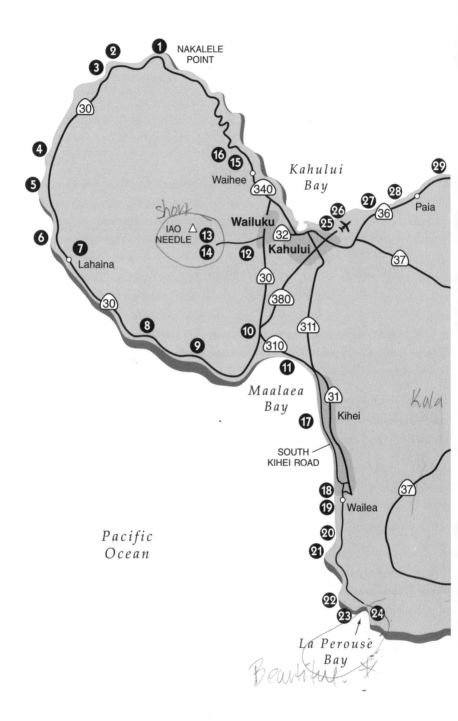

NAKALELE POINT

Kahului Bay

Waihee

Wailuku

IAO NEEDLE

Kahului

Paia

Lahaina

Maalaea Bay

Kihei

SOUTH KIHEI ROAD

Wailea

Pacific Ocean

La Perouse Bay

Beautiful

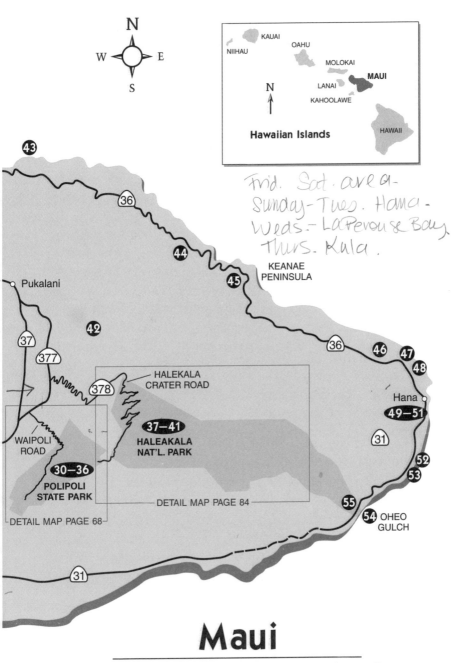

Frid. Sat. area- Sunday-Tues. Hana- Weds.- La Perouse Bay, Thurs. Kula.

Maui
MAP OF THE HIKES

Hike 1
Nakalele Blowhole

Hiking distance: 1 mile round trip
Hiking time: 1 hour
Elevation gain: 200 feet
Maps: U.S.G.S. Napili
       Maui Recreation Map

Summary of hike: This place is pure magic. The Nakalele Blowhole is at the desolate north tip of Maui by a lighthouse beacon on the east edge of Nakalele Point. The blowhole is in a small cove with rough, turbulent surf. The cove is surrounded by layered, wind-sculpted lava formations and tidepools. At the trailhead is a surrealistic open field covered with hundreds of cairns. The trail passes the light beacon before crossing the beautifully carved lava rock shelf, passing tidepools en route to the blowhole. The blowhole erupts as incoming waves blast air and water through a hole from an underwater sea cave. The water will spurt more vigorously during high tide.

Driving directions: From Lahaina, drive 16 miles north on Highway 30 to the north tip of the island. Park on the left (ocean side) of the road at a large open area marked by a sign.

Hiking directions: Follow the old jeep road/trail as it winds into the ironwood tree grove. Continue the gradual descent east past the Coast Guard beacon and down to the ocean. The path ends beyond the beacon. Walk out over the lava shelf past tidepools towards the farthest point. The blowhole is in a cove east of Nakalele Point. If you have any difficulty locating the blowhole, listen for the frequent eruptions. Explore the amazing jagged landscape along your own route.

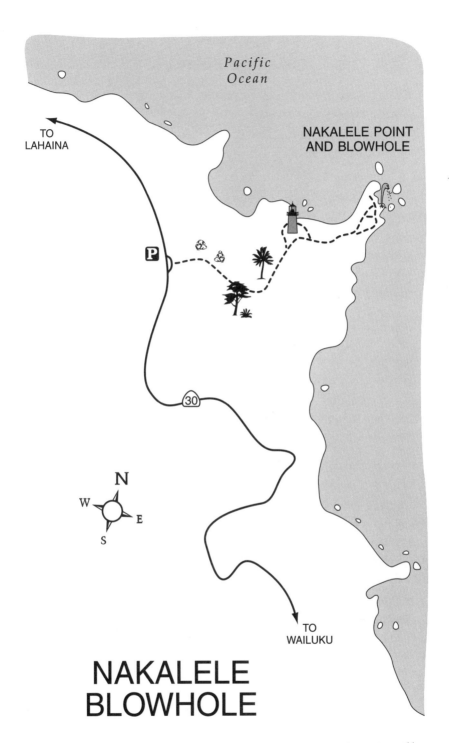

Pacific
Ocean

TO
LAHAINA

NAKALELE POINT
AND BLOWHOLE

P

30

N
W E
S

TO
WAILUKU

NAKALELE BLOWHOLE

Hike 2
Lipoa Point

Hiking distance: 1 mile round trip
Hiking time: 30 minutes
Elevation gain: 100 feet
Maps: U.S.G.S. Napili

Summary of hike: At Lipoa Point are tidepools, hollowed out caves, natural arches and clear snorkeling and soaking pools. The point is at the northwest tip of Kulaokaea, a large plateau used for cultivating pineapples. The broad, flat plateau, known locally as "Golf Links," was the site of a golf course in the 1940s. A few eroded trails also lead down the steep cliffs into small pocket beaches in Honolua Bay, a designated marine sanctuary.

Driving directions: From Lahaina, drive 11.8 miles north on Highway 30 to a wide red dirt road on the left, between mile markers 33 and 34. The highway curves to the right at the turnoff. Turn left and follow the road along the west side of Lipoa Point through pineapple fields. The end of the road is at 0.3 miles. Along the way are several pullouts on the left that lead to steep trails descending the cliffs into Honolua Bay.

Hiking directions: From the pullouts before the end of the road, the path zigzags down the steep cliffs to a knoll and trail junction. The left fork leads down to the north end of Honolua Bay. To the right, an equally steep trail descends into a small pocket cove. Use caution and good judgement to descend.

From the main trail at the end of the road, follow the red dirt path along the perimeter of the plateau towards Lipoa Point. Several side paths descend to the left. At 0.3 miles are the remains of an old rock wall, the site of the golf course clubhouse. Near the wall is a Norfolk pine grove and a trail junction. Bear left and descend the hill towards Lipoa Point. Various paths crisscross the lava rock point that overlooks the jagged coastline and interesting rock formations. Explore along your own route.

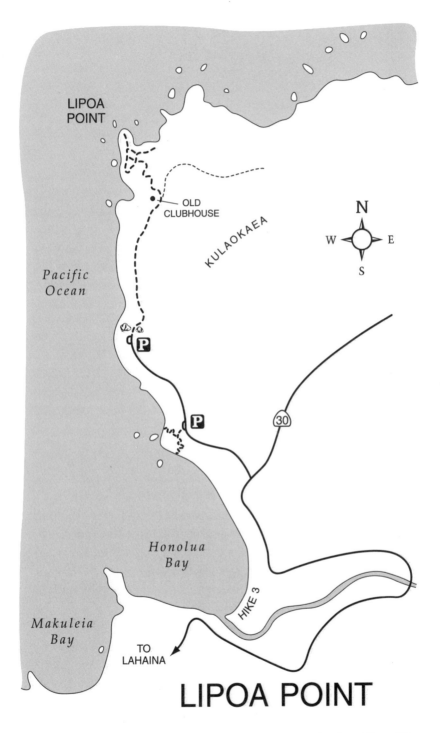

LIPOA POINT

LIPOA
POINT

OLD
CLUBHOUSE

KULAOKAEA

N
W   E
S

Pacific
Ocean

P

P

30

Honolua
Bay

HIKE 3

Makuleia
Bay

TO
LAHAINA

LIPOA POINT

Hike 3
Honolua Bay

Hiking distance: 0.5 miles round trip
Hiking time: 30 minutes
Elevation gain: 50 feet
Maps: U.S.G.S. Napili
       Maui Recreation Map

Summary of hike: Honolua Bay, a designated marine sanctuary, is a deep circular bay backed by a lush tropical forest. It is a popular snorkeling, diving and surfing destination. The beach is primarily covered with boulders and scattered sand patches and is bordered by high sea cliffs. Above the bay, atop the plateau, are pineapple fields that lead to Lipoa Point (Hike 2). A trail leads through the dense forest to the rocky shoreline, where the intermittent Honolua Stream empties into the bay.

Driving directions: From Lahaina, drive 11 miles north on Highway 30 to signed pullouts on the left side of the road, between mile markers 32 and 33. The pullouts are just before the sharp left curve in the highway, where the road begins to descend and cross a one-lane bridge.

Hiking directions: From the sharp left bend in the highway, walk down the path past the red metal trailhead gate. Access to the bay crosses through private land owned by the Maui Land and Pineapple Company. The signage at the trailhead requests that you stay on the trail to the bay. Continue down the wide path, an old jeep road, through the shade of the tropical forest. Cross a rocky wash, arriving at the center of Honolua Bay by an old boat ramp. Beachcomb along the rocky shoreline, choosing your own turnaround spot.

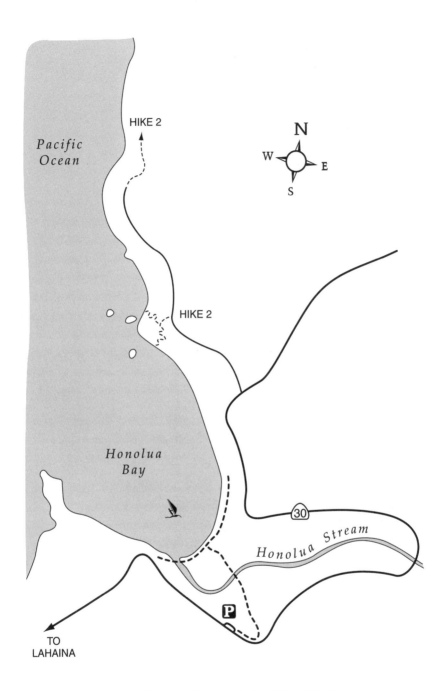

HONOLUA BAY

Hike 4
D.T. Fleming Beach Park
to Makaluapuna Point

Hiking distance: 1.5 miles round trip
Hiking time: 1 hour
Elevation gain: Level
Maps: U.S.G.S. Napili
　　　　Maui Recreation Map

Summary of hike: Fleming Beach Park is a crescent-shaped beach protected by two rocky headlands at Honokahua Bay. Honokahua Stream empties into the bay in a grove of ironwood and kiawe trees. Makaluapuna Point is the lava rock peninsula jutting a quarter mile into the ocean, separating Honokahua Bay from Oneloa Bay. A ridge of jagged trachyte formations known as "Dragon's Teeth" extend to the point. The hike begins at the beach and leads across the lava formations to the point, exploring tidepools and overlooking the crashing surf. East Molokai is visible across the Pailolo Channel.

Driving directions: From Lahaina, drive about 10 miles north on Highway 30 to the north end of Kapalua. Turn left to the D.T. Fleming Beach Park parking lot.

Hiking directions: From the sandy beach, walk to the left (west) along the crescent of sand. The sand ends at the foot of Makaluapuna Point. Begin climbing the field of lava rocks towards the distinct trachyte formations. Continue along the side of the jagged ridge, working your way to Makaluapuna Point. (The Kapalua Golf Course boundary eliminates direct access into Oneloa Bay.) After exploring this magnificent area, return the way you came.

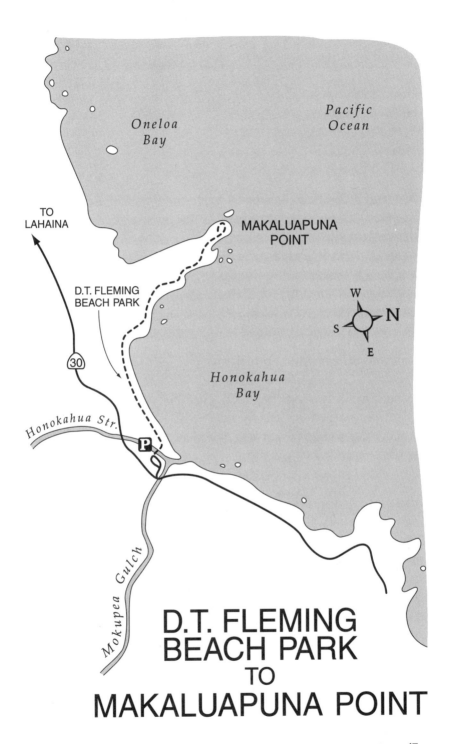

Oneloa
Bay

*Pacific
Ocean*

MAKALUAPUNA
POINT

TO
LAHAINA

D.T. FLEMING
BEACH PARK

30

Honokahua Str.

*Honokahua
Bay*

P

Mokupea Gulch

D.T. FLEMING
BEACH PARK
TO
MAKALUAPUNA POINT

Hike 5
Kapalua "Fleming" Beach

Hiking distance: 0.8 miles round trip
Hiking time: 30 minutes
Elevation gain: Level
Maps: U.S.G.S. Napili
Maui Recreation Map

Summary of hike: Kapalua Beach, also known as Fleming Beach, is a popular swimming and snorkeling site. The picturesque crescent-shaped beach is protected by a coral reef and lined with palms. The bay is bordered by a rocky point to the south and Kaekaha, a peninsula separating the beach from Namalu Bay to the north. The trail crosses a luxury resort complex at the north end of the bay to the lava rock peninsula. The views extend across the Pailolo Channel to East Molokai.

Driving directions: From Lahaina, drive 9 miles north on Highway 30 to the signed Kapalua turnoff, just past the 30 mile marker. Turn left and drive to the end of Napilihau Street at the T-junction with Lower Honoapiilani Road. Turn right and continue 0.8 miles to the parking lot on the left, just past the Napili Kai Resort.

Hiking directions: Walk toward the beach on the paved beach access past the Napili Kai Resort on the left. Descend a set of steps on the left, and walk through the tunnel, entering picturesque Kapalua Bay. The paved path parallels the back side of the sandy beach along a row of palm trees. At the north end of the bay near the swimming pool, leave the path and cross the large grassy knoll on the left towards Kaekaha Point. At the point, cross the lava rock, exploring along your own route.

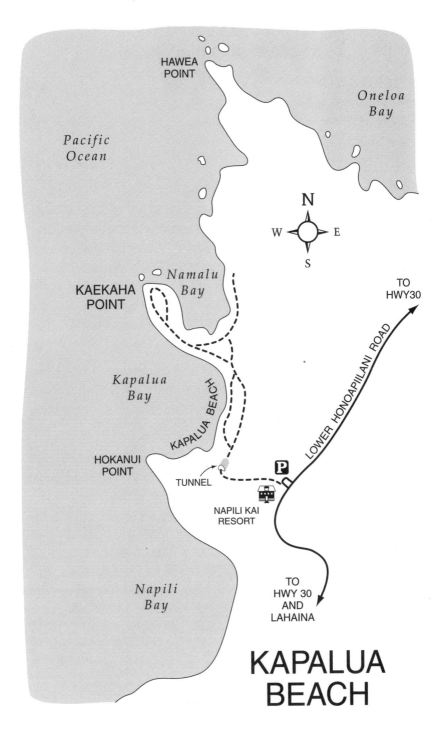

HAWEA
POINT

*Oneloa
Bay*

*Pacific
Ocean*

N

W E

S

*Namalu
Bay*

KAEKAHA
POINT

*Kapalua
Bay*

KAPALUA BEACH

HOKANUI
POINT

TUNNEL

P

TO
HWY30

LOWER HONOAPIILANI ROAD

NAPILI KAI
RESORT

TO
HWY 30
AND
LAHAINA

*Napili
Bay*

KAPALUA
BEACH

Hike 6
Hanakaoo Beach Park
to Wahikuli State Park

Hiking distance: 2.2 miles round trip
Hiking time: 1 hour
Elevation gain: Level
Maps: U.S.G.S. Lahaina
       Maui Recreation Map

Summary of hike: Both of these parks border a long uninterrupted stretch of golden sand between Kaanapali and Lahaina. A path connects the southern end of Hanakaoo Beach Park with Wahikuli State Park. This hike follows the walking path through both beach parks past grassy picnic areas and shady kiawe and palm tree groves. With easy access from Lahaina and excellent beach and picnic facilities, the parks are popular swimming, snorkeling and picnic sites. To the north, the beach is adjacent to the Kaanapali resorts.

Driving directions: From Lahaina, drive 2.4 miles north on Highway 30 to the signed Hanakaoo Beach Park entrance on the left and park.

Hiking directions: To the north, the beach is bordered by kiawe trees. Take the paved path to the south, in the direction of Lahaina, through a shady picnic area. The paved path becomes a red dirt trail which parallels the shoreline past several pockets of sand divided by black lava rocks. At 0.4 miles, cross a grassy area dotted with palms and kiawe trees. The path narrows and continues south, entering Wahikuli State Park. Cross the grassy park above the sandy beach to the south end of the park at Lahaina, a short distance before Front Street. This is the turnaround spot.

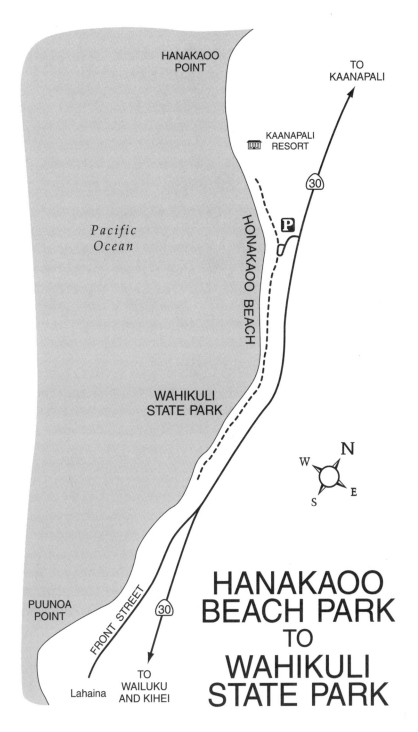

HANAKAOO
POINT

TO
KAANAPALI

KAANAPALI
RESORT

(30)

P

*Pacific
Ocean*

HONAKAOO BEACH

WAHIKULI
STATE PARK

N
W E
S

HANAKAOO
BEACH PARK
TO
WAHIKULI
STATE PARK

PUUNOA
POINT

FRONT STREET

(30)

Lahaina

TO
WAILUKU
AND KIHEI

Hike 7
Lahaina "L" and David Malo's Grave
Hiking permit needed from Pioneer Mill Co. (808) 661-3129
Office (en route to trailhead) at 380 Lahainaluna Road

Hiking distance: 5 miles round trip
Hiking time: 3 hours
Elevation gain: 1,750 feet
Maps: U.S.G.S. Lahaina

Summary of hike: If you like steep hikes, this is the hike for you. The trail to the Lahaina "L" is a direct route up the mountain, with little finesse. The "L" is a 30-foot long engraving in the mountainside above Lahaina. David Malo's stone-covered grave, above the "L," is a monument with plaques and tributes to the 1800s scholar and humanitarian. From the grave and the "L" are great views of Lahaina, Kaanapali, the western coastline and the islands of Molokai and Lanai.

Driving directions: From downtown Lahaina, turn east (inland) on Lahainaluna Road near the tall cement smokestacks. Drive 0.2 miles to the Pioneer Mill office on the right. After receiving your permit, continue 1.2 miles and turn right into the football field parking lot.

Hiking directions: Walk up the steps to the asphalt road. Follow the road to the right a hundred yards, and bear right alongside a row of mango trees and a water flume to a metal gate. Twenty yards beyond the gate, take the trail uphill to the left, following the power poles. At the top of the foothill along the base of Mount Ball, follow the cane road to the right. When the road bends to the right, watch on the left for eucalyptus trees painted orange. Take this narrow footpath left, following the orange markers through the eucalyptus grove, to a trail split at a fenceline. Continue straight ahead through the thick brush on the steep uphill path, climbing unmercifully to the "L." After resting and enjoying the great views, head up to the top of the "L." A short distance beyond is David Malo's grave.

To return, take the trail to the right, heading south for a more gradual descent. The trail is marked with orange ribbons and exits behind an old abandoned house by a cascading stream and waterwheel. Walk through the house and descend the porch steps to the cane road. Bear right and follow the road. Take any of several roads to the left downhill to the next intersecting road. Bear to the right, completing the loop near the power poles, and return to the trailhead.

MALO'S GRAVE
(2,261 feet)

L

Paupau Ditch

N
E
W
S

Piilani Ditch

Kahana Stream

HIGH SCHOOL

P

FOOTBALL FIELD

Lahainaluna Ditch

LAHAINALUNA ROAD

TO LAHAINA

LAHAINA "L"
AND
DAVID MALO'S GRAVE

Hike 8
Olowalu Petroglyphs

Hiking distance: 1 mile round trip
Hiking time: 1 hour
Elevation gain: 100 feet
Maps: U.S.G.S. Olowalu
Map of Maui—The Valley Isle

Summary of hike: The Olowalu Petroglyphs are ancient Hawaiian petroglyphs (images chiseled into the rock surface) depicting humans and animals. The 300-year-old stone carvings are engraved into the face of Kilea, a volcanic cinder cone in the V-shaped Olowalu Valley. The trail follows an ancient Hawaiian route that crossed the Olowalu Valley into the Iao Valley. This area is now privately owned, and public access ends at the petroglyphs.

Driving directions: From Lahaina, drive 6 miles south on Highway 30 to the Olowalu Store on the inland (left) side of the highway, near mile marker 15. Turn left and park near but not in front of the store.

From Wailuku, drive south on Highway 30. Curve west around McGregor Point towards Lahaina, reaching the Olowalu Store on the right at about 15 miles.

Hiking directions: Walk behind the Olowalu Store and down the cane road to the water tank. Follow the dirt road for a half mile through the sugar cane field into the Olowalu Valley towards Kilea, the volcanic hill. As the road approaches the distinct cinder cone, human figures carved into the face of the west hillside will be visible. Unstable remnants of walkways, railings and an observation platform remain. After viewing the petroglyphs, you must return along the same route. Further access on the privately owned road is prohibited.

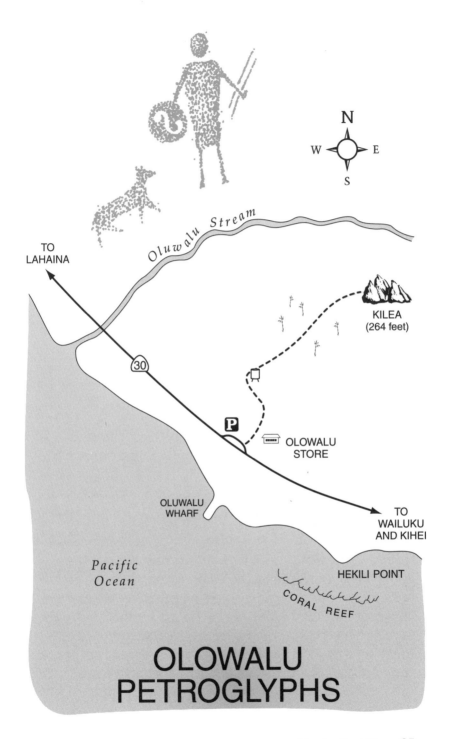

OLOWALU
PETROGLYPHS

Hike 9
Lahaina Pali Trail
from the Ukumehame (West) Trailhead

Hiking distance: 5 miles round trip
Hiking time: 3 hours
Elevation gain: 1,600 feet
Maps: U.S.G.S. Maalaea
      The Lahaina Pali Trail Guide

map
next page

Summary of hike: The Lahaina Pali Trail is an old Hawaiian horse and foot trail built in the early 1800s. The trail was used as a more direct route across the arid southern slopes of the West Maui Mountains, connecting Lahaina and Olowalu with Maalaea and Wailuku. There are two trailheads that zigzag up the mountain, crossing ridges and gullies to the 1,600-foot ridge. The interpretive trail passes rock outcroppings, ancient stone walls and offers panoramic coastal vistas of Lanai, Kahoolawe, Haleakala and the Molokini Islands. This hike begins from the Ukumehame (West) Trailhead and can be combined with Hike 10 for a one-way, 5-mile shuttle hike.

Driving directions: The signed trailhead is on the inland side of the Kahekili Highway (30) between the 10 and 11 mile marker. It is 4 miles west of the Maalaea Harbor and a half mile past the Lahaina Tunnel. It is 10 miles southeast of downtown Lahaina. Turn inland and park in the trailhead parking area under the shade of the kiawe trees.

Hiking directions: Walk through the grove and up the steps to the mouth of Manawaipueo Gulch. Bear right on the asphalt road, the old, winding carriage route used before the Highway 30 tunnel was built. Head to the signed footpath 60 yards ahead. Bear left on the Lahaina Pali Trail, ascending the mountain to the west edge of Kamaohi Gulch. The highway tunnel can be seen at the mouth of the gulch. Follow the cliff's edge to the head of the gulch and cross. Watch for a cave on the left. The trail heads up and crosses Mokumana Gulch at one mile and

Opunaha Gulch at 1.4 miles. A water trough for cattle is on the right. The path levels out after crossing Makahuna Gulch. Views extend down the Kihei coastline to the offshore islands and the towering Haleakala. Cross Kaalaina Gulch to the open expanse of Pohakuloa. Descend to the base of Manawainui Gulch to the shade of a wiliwili tree at 1.9 miles. Climb back out on the switchbacks to the high point of the trail on the windswept ridge by signpost 10. This is our turnaround spot. To hike further, the trail descends to the Maalaea Trailhead (Hike 10).

Hike 10
Lahaina Pali Trail
from the Maalaea (East) Trailhead

Hiking distance: 5 miles round trip
Hiking time: 3 hours
Elevation gain: 1,600 feet
Maps: U.S.G.S. Maalaea
      The Lahaina Pali Trail Guide

map
next page

Summary of hike: The Lahaina Pali Trail is an old route across the southern end of the West Maui Mountains, connecting Lahaina with Maalaea and Wailuku. The serpentine horse and foot trail was hand built in the early 1800s. The path crosses numerous ridges and gullies, reaching the 1,600 foot summit on a windswept ridge. This hike begins from the Maalaea (East) Trailhead and can be combined with Hike 9 for a one-way, 5-mile shuttle hike. The interpretive trail passes rock outcroppings, ancient stone walls and trail paving stones while offering access to sweeping coastal and island views.

Driving directions: The signed trailhead is on the Kahekili Highway (30) at the north end of Kihei by Maalaea. The trailhead is 0.1 mile south of the Kuihelani Highway (380) and 0.2 miles north of the North Kihei Road (310) on the west side of the road. Turn west off Highway 30 to the signed trailhead gate. Drive through the gate, closing the gate, and continue 0.2 miles to a junction. Bear left and follow the trail signs. Cross through another gate, driving 0.6 miles to the parking area on the right.

Hiking directions: Walk through the entrance gate, and follow the rock-lined path through groves of kiawe trees. Begin climbing up the steep path, zigzagging up the ridge of the mountain while leaving the shade behind. Views unfold of Maui and the surrounding islands. Traverse the mountainside, crossing numerous dry gullies. Continue steadily uphill. The trail levels out on Kealaloloa Ridge. Curve around the ridge to the McGregor Point Jeep Trail, an unpaved road at the edge of Malalowaiaole Gulch. Take the road to the left, crossing the gulch to a signed junction. Leave the road and take the footpath to the right. Climb up the rock steps to the high point of the trail on a ridge by signpost 10. This is our turnaround spot. To hike further, the trail descends to the Ukumehame Trailhead (Hike 9).

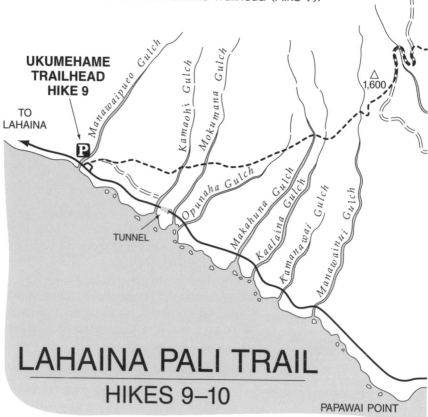

UKUMEHAME
TRAILHEAD
HIKE 9

TO
LAHAINA

Manawaipueo Gulch

Kamaohi Gulch

Mokumana Gulch

Opunaha Gulch

Makahuna Gulch

Kaalaina Gulch

Kamanawai Gulch

Manawainui Gulch

△
1,600

TUNNEL

LAHAINA PALI TRAIL
HIKES 9–10

PAPAWAI POINT

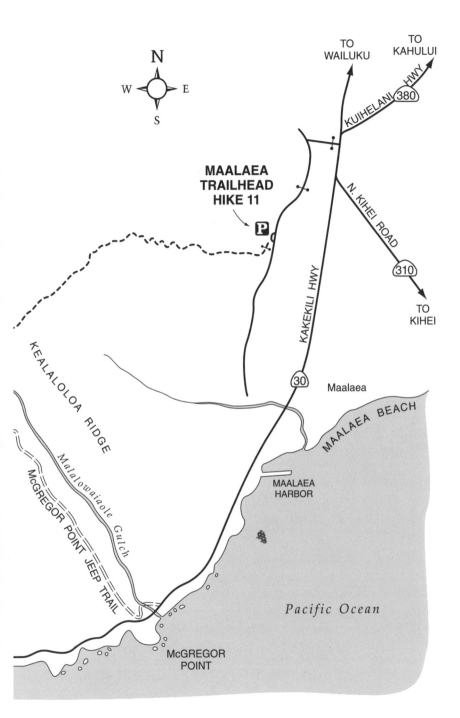

Hike 11
Maalaea Beach

Hiking distance: 4.8 miles round trip
Hiking time: 2.5 hours
Elevation gain: Level
Maps: U.S.G.S. Maalaea
Maui Recreation Map

Summary of hike: Maalaea Beach is on the sandy south shore of the isthmus between the two mountains that form Maui. The curving white sand beach strand stretches for three miles, from Maalaea Boat Harbor to North Kihei by Sugar Beach. The beach strand is backed by Kealia Pond, a 700-acre national wildlife refuge. The wide, uninterrupted hard packed sand has made Maalaea Beach a favorite walking and jogging area. Due to late morning and early afternoon winds, the beach is best enjoyed in the early morning and late afternoon or evening.

Driving directions: Maalaea Beach is at the north end of Kihei. From the junction of the North Kihei Road (310) and the Kahekili Highway (30) drive 2 miles southeast on Highway 310 towards Kihei to the parking pullout on the right. It is across the highway from the Kealia Pond, a wildlife refuge.

Hiking directions: To the right (west) the beach strand quickly moves away from the highway and follows the shoreline for 1.2 miles to the Maalaea Village Condos near the boat harbor. To the left (east) the path follows the shoreline parallel to Highway 310 for 1.2 miles, ending at more oceanfront condominiums. The beach is backed by sand dunes and kiawe trees, which act as a buffer between the beach and the highway.

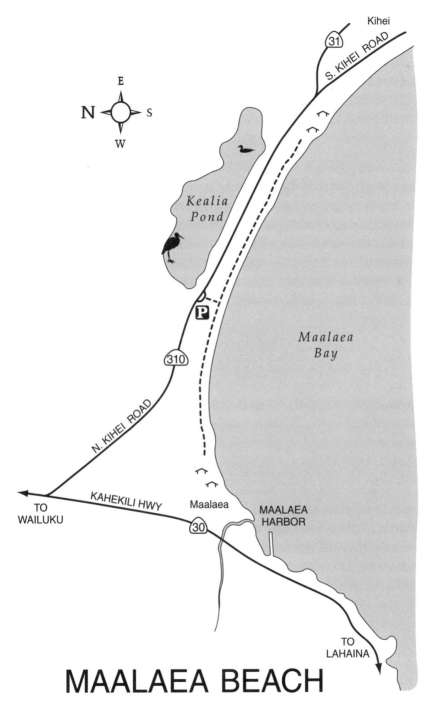

MAALAEA BEACH

Hike 12
Kapilau Ridge Trail to Wailuku Cross

Hiking distance: 1.8 miles round trip
Hiking time: 1 hour
Elevation gain: 1,000 feet
Maps: U.S.G.S. Wailuku

Summary of hike: Kapilau Ridge, at the west end of Wailuku, separates the Iao Valley from the Waikapu Valley. This ridge trail is a short, steep unmaintained footpath directly up the ridge to a large wooden cross overlooking Wailuku. The cross was originally built by students of St. Anthony High School in 1956 and is still maintained by the students. A ladder climbs up the cross to panoramic views extending from Paia and the Waihee Valley to Kihei and Wailea.

Driving directions: From High Street in downtown Wailuku, turn west (towards the mountains) on Main Street/Highway 32. Go a half mile towards the Iao Needle to a road split. Stay left a quarter mile to telephone pole #5 at a left bend in the road. Park in the small pullout on the right. There is additional parking about 20 yards back down the road on the left.

Hiking directions: Take the unsigned footpath on the right side of telephone pole #5, and enter the shade of the ironwood tree forest. Follow the steep path west up Kapilau Ridge as it rises high above Iao Valley. As you climb, the trail passes numerous overlooks. Turn around to notice the great coastal and inland views to the north and east. Near the large wooden cross, the trail emerges from the forest cover. A ladder attached to the cross offers sweeping vistas. This is our turn-around spot.

To hike further, the trail steepens and, without mercy, climbs up the ridge to an overlook of the Iao Valley and Iao Needle (Hike 13).

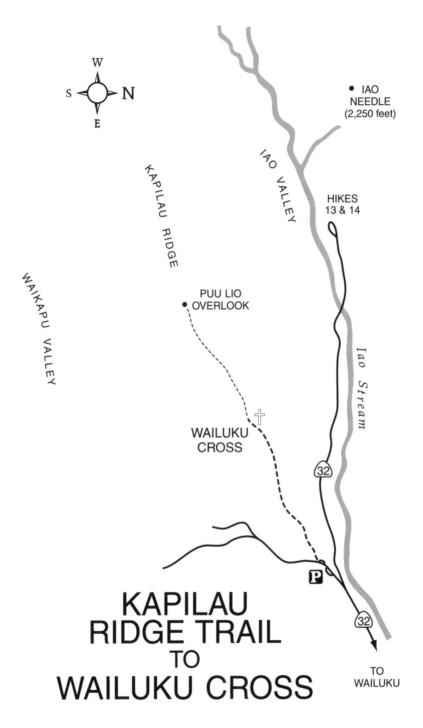

KAPILAU
RIDGE TRAIL
TO
WAILUKU CROSS

W
N
S
E

IAO
NEEDLE
(2,250 feet)

IAO VALLEY

HIKES
13 & 14

KAPILAU RIDGE

WAIKAPU VALLEY

PUU LIO
OVERLOOK

Iao Stream

WAILUKU
CROSS

32

P

32

TO
WAILUKU

Hike 13
Iao Needle Overlook and Botanical Garden
Iao Valley State Park

Hiking distance: 0.6 miles round trip
Hiking time: 30 minutes
Elevation gain: 150 feet
Maps: U.S.G.S. Wailuku

Summary of hike: Iao Valley, an ancient sacred site and spiritual center, sits in a rich green chasm in the West Maui Mountains above the town of Wailuku. The six-acre state park is home of Kukaemoku, commonly referred to as the Iao Needle, a moss-covered 2,250-foot basalt mantle that sharply rises 1,200 feet from the valley floor (cover photo). The Iao Needle Overlook is a roofed pavilion with benches overlooking Wailuku, the Iao Valley, Iao Needle and the precipitous steep valley walls. A paved nature trail curves through a tropical botanic garden that borders the banks of the Iao Stream. The gardens are landscaped with native and introduced plants.

Driving directions: Iao Valley State Park is at the west end of Wailuku. From downtown, turn west (towards the mountains) on Main Street/Highway 32. Drive 2.8 miles to the end of the road and park in the lot.

Hiking directions: Hike up the paved path past the restrooms towards the bridge crossing over a tributary of Iao Stream. Before crossing, take the interpretive nature trail to the left, descending into the botanical garden. Follow the paved path, exploring the gardens and ponds. The trail loops at the southern end along Iao Stream. After strolling through the gardens, return to the main trail by the bridge. Cross the bridge over the stream and curve left on the paved path to a trail split. The left fork leads to the Streamside Trail (Hike 14). Take the right fork and ascend over a hundred steps to the Iao Needle Overlook shelter at the end of the trail.

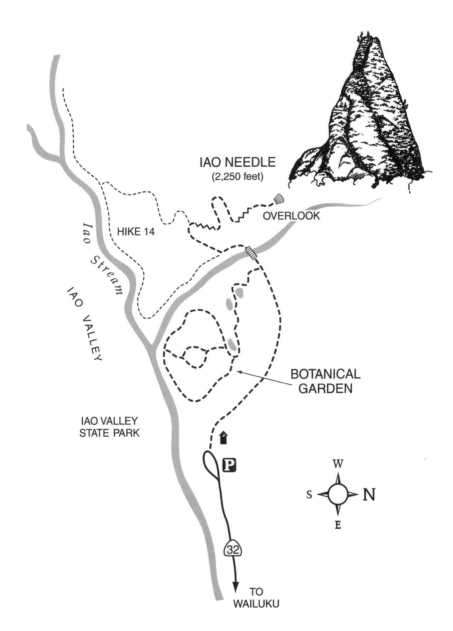

IAO NEEDLE
(2,250 feet)

OVERLOOK

HIKE 14

Iao Stream

IAO VALLEY

BOTANICAL
GARDEN

IAO VALLEY
STATE PARK

P

W
S — N
E

32

TO
WAILUKU

IAO NEEDLE OVERLOOK
AND
BOTANICAL GARDEN

Hike 14
Streamside Trail
Iao Valley State Park

Hiking distance: 1 mile round trip
Hiking time: 30 minutes
Elevation gain: 200 feet
Maps: U.S.G.S. Wailuku

Summary of hike: The Streamside Trail meanders through the lush stream-fed chasm and dramatic landscape of Iao Valley State Park, an ancient spiritual center in the West Maui Mountains. Waters from a network of tributary streams emerge from the folds of Iao Valley, converging inside the park to form Iao Stream. The trail crosses a footbridge over a stream and winds through a shady tropical forest to tumbling cascades, small waterfalls and natural pools.

Driving directions: Iao Valley State Park is at the west end of Wailuku. From downtown, turn west (towards the mountains) on Main Street/Highway 32. Drive 2.8 miles to the end of the road and park in the lot.

Hiking directions: Walk up the paved path past the restrooms to a bridge crossing a tributary of Iao Stream. From the bridge is an excellent view of the 2,250-foot Iao Needle (cover photo). After crossing, curve left to a trail split. The right fork leads up to the Iao Needle Overlook (Hike 13). Bear left and descend to the Iao Stream. Follow the paved path along the stream as the cascading whitewater tumbles over rocks. When the paved path loops to the right, away from the stream, watch for a streamside footpath heading west. Follow the footpath upstream into the damp forest, passing cascades to several pools. Use caution as the mossy rocks are slippery. Return to the paved path. Take the left fork and ascend the hill through guava and yellow ginger trees to a junction. The left fork climbs steps to the Iao Needle Overlook (Hike 13). Stay to the right and complete the loop. Return to the left.

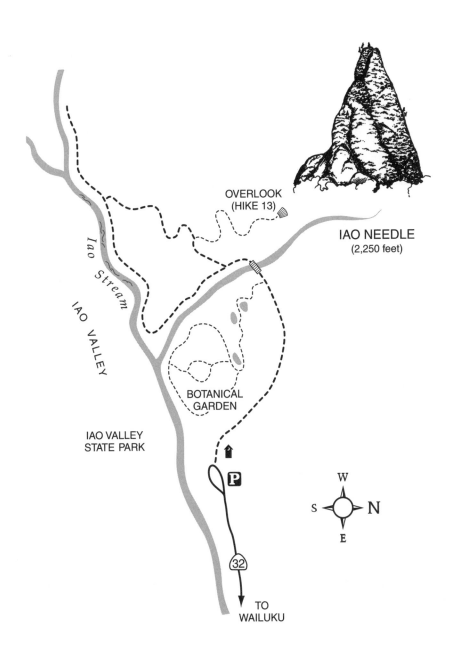

OVERLOOK
(HIKE 13)

IAO NEEDLE
(2,250 feet)

Iao Stream

IAO VALLEY

BOTANICAL
GARDEN

IAO VALLEY
STATE PARK

P

W
S   N
E

32

TO
WAILUKU

STREAMSIDE TRAIL

Hike 15
Waihee Valley

Hiking permit needed from Wailuku Agribusiness
Call (808) 244-9570

Hiking distance: 4 miles round trip
Hiking time: 2 hours
Elevation gain: 300 feet
Maps: U.S.G.S. Wailuku

Summary of hike: Waihee Valley is a narrow, stream-fed canyon with steep vertical walls. The trail winds gently through the lush, tropical rain forest and crosses two long swinging bridges over the Waihee River. The hike winds up the canyon past bamboo forests, huge banyan trees and views of narrow waterfalls cascading over the steep canyon walls. Be aware that flash flooding is possible. If it is raining, do not hike in this area.

Driving directions: From the intersection of Main Street and Market Street in downtown Wailuku, head north on Market Street. Veer to the left onto Highway 340 and drive through the town of Waihee. From the Waihee School on the left, continue 0.5 miles to the signed Waihee Valley Road and turn left. Drive 0.5 miles to the end of the road and park.

Hiking directions: At the end of Waihee Valley Road, walk on the service road to the right (west). As you pass some abandoned cars, water can be heard flowing through an irrigation ditch. Follow the irrigation stream through the lush forest as it flows in and out of tunnels dug into the cliffs. At one mile, cross the first swinging bridge. The riverbed may be dry depending on where the water is being diverted from the irrigation system. Crossing the bridges is great fun regardless of the water level. After crossing, bear left to a second bridge. Continue up the canyon to where the trail fords the river. This is a good turnaround spot if you do not wish to wade through the water. To hike further, the trail fords the river a second time, reaching the dam and swimming holes in less than a half mile.

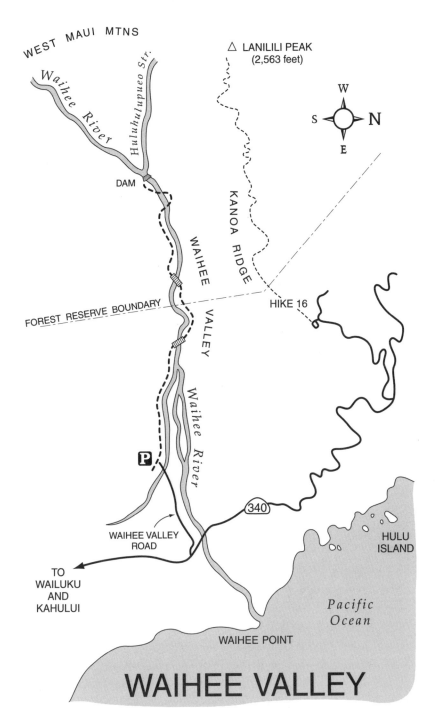

WEST MAUI MTNS

Waihee River

Huluhulupueo Str.

△ LANILILI PEAK
(2,563 feet)

DAM

KANOA RIDGE

WAIHEE VALLEY

FOREST RESERVE BOUNDARY

HIKE 16

Waihee River

P

340

WAIHEE VALLEY
ROAD

TO
WAILUKU
AND
KAHULUI

HULU
ISLAND

Pacific
Ocean

WAIHEE POINT

WAIHEE VALLEY

Hike 16
Waihee Ridge

Hiking distance: 4.5 miles round trip
Hiking time: 2.5 hours
Elevation gain: 1,500 feet
Maps: U.S.G.S. Wailuku
   Island of Maui Recreation Map

Summary of hike: The Waihee Ridge Trail begins in the rolling pasturelands of the West Maui Mountains. The trail climbs the windward slopes along the crest of Kanoa Ridge overlooking the Waihee Canyon (Hike 15). The path leads through the heavily foliated rainforest to Lanilili Peak. There are incredible views along the way of the canyons, mountain ridges and coastline. The trail is well maintained but portions are wet and muddy.

Driving directions: From the intersection of Main Street and Market Street in downtown Wailuku, head north on Market Street. Veer to the left onto Highway 340 and drive through the town of Waihee. From the Waihee School on the left, continue 2.7 miles to the signed Camp Maluhia turnoff and turn left. Drive 0.8 miles to the grassy parking area on the left by the vehicle gate.

Hiking directions: Hike west past the trailhead gate, and proceed 0.2 miles through the pastureland. Walk up the steep concrete right-of-way road towards a water tower on the right. Take the signed grassy footpath uphill to the left. At a quarter mile, cross through the forest reserve gate. Continue uphill through the rainforest to an overlook on a saddle at 0.5 miles. Long switchbacks lead up the mountain to a second saddle with great views into Waihee Valley and the Maui isthmus. More switchbacks ascend the mountain to a narrow ridge. At 1.5 miles, the trail levels and crosses a meadow towards Lanilili Peak. Switchbacks lead up to the 2,563-foot summit, a grassy hilltop with a picnic table at trail's end. After viewing the massive ridges and deep valleys, return by retracing your steps.

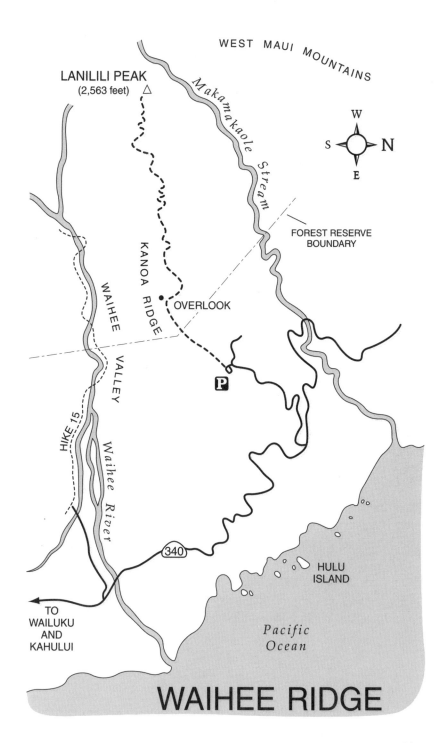

WEST MAUI MOUNTAINS

LANILILI PEAK
(2,563 feet) △

Makamakaole Stream

W
S ✦ N
E

FOREST RESERVE
BOUNDARY

KANOA RIDGE

OVERLOOK

WAIHEE VALLEY

Waihee River

HIKE 15

P

340

HULU
ISLAND

TO
WAILUKU
AND
KAHULUI

*Pacific
Ocean*

WAIHEE RIDGE

Hike 17
Kamaole Beaches 1, 2 and 3

Hiking distance: 2 miles round trip
Hiking time: 1 hour
Elevation gain: Near level
Maps: U.S.G.S. Puu O Kali

Summary of hike: The Kamaole Beaches are three separate but adjacent beach parks bordering South Kihei Road. All three white sand beaches are connected by low grassy sea cliffs and are bordered by rocky promontories. Kamaole 3, the shortest of the three beach pockets, is backed by a large tree-shaded grassy knoll.

Driving directions: On South Kihei Road in Kihei, the signed Kamaole I parking lot is on the 2200 block, across from the Chevron station. The street numbers increase heading south. Park on the right in the oceanfront parking lot. Additional parking is available on the inland side of the highway north of the Chevron station.

Hiking directions: Walk a short distance north to the lava rock point and palm-covered bluff. Return south along the beach 0.4 miles to the south end of Kamaole 1. Head up the grassy knoll and cross the bluffs past the Royal Mauian Hotel, overlooking the rocky promontory. Descend onto the white sand beach of Kamaole 2. Stroll across the beach strand, which is backed with palm trees. At the south end of Kamaole 2 is a rock jetty at 0.7 miles. Walk up the hill to the grassy knoll above Kamaole 3. Follow the parkland knoll or walk along the beach strand, each ending at one mile. To extend the hike, several paths cross the oceanfront bluffs to the Kihei boat ramp at 1.2 miles.

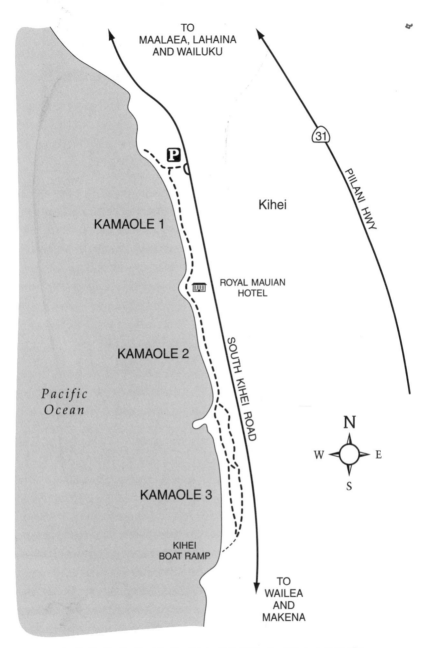

TO
MAALAEA, LAHAINA
AND WAILUKU

P

(31)

Kihei

PIILANI HWY

KAMAOLE 1

ROYAL MAUIAN
HOTEL

KAMAOLE 2

*Pacific
Ocean*

SOUTH KIHEI ROAD

N

W — E

S

KAMAOLE 3

KIHEI
BOAT RAMP

TO
WAILEA
AND
MAKENA

KAMAOLE BEACHES
1–2–3

Hike 18
Wailea Oceanfront Boardwalk
Keawakapu, Mokapu, Ulua, Wailea and Polo Beaches

Hiking distance: 4 miles round trip
Hiking time: 2 hours
Elevation gain: Level
Maps: U.S.G.S. Makena

Summary of hike: The Wailea Boardwalk follows two miles of coastline fronting a string of world class resorts. Each of the five public beaches have differing characteristics; all are great swimming and snorkeling sites. The lush, landscaped grounds of the resorts behind the beaches are also a treasure to explore. The boardwalk connects the five beach coves, which are separated by wide stretches of lava rock promontories with tidepools. The Hawaiian Coastal Gardens on Wailea Point are a half-mile long with over 60 native plants. Throughout the hike are great views of Molokini Island, Kahoolawe and Lanai.

Driving directions: At the south end of Kihei, the South Kihei Road ends. Where the main road curves left at the signed entrance to Wailea on Okolani Drive, take the right fork 0.2 miles to the Keawakapu Beach parking lot at the road's end.

Hiking directions: Walk down the steps to Keawakapu Beach. Bear left between the kiawe trees on the sand dunes and the oceanfront lava rocks. Follow the sandy strand 0.2 miles to the paved walking path in front of the Wailea Beach Resort at Mokapu Beach. Wind through the landscaped gardens with spur paths leading to the oceanfront and tidepools. The boardwalk continues to Wailea Elua Village and Ulua Beach along the weaving contours of the landscaped grounds. Cross the lava formations and tidepools to the Outrigger Wailea Resort, then the Grand Wailea Resort fronted by Wailea Beach. Head up the grassy bluffs to the Hawaiian Coastal Gardens. Cross the footbridge over the lush gully to the rocky cliffs of Wailea Point. Around the point, pass the remains of an ancient Hawaiian home from the 1300s. At Polo Beach, the trail ends at a small park and the beach parking lot on Old Makena Road.

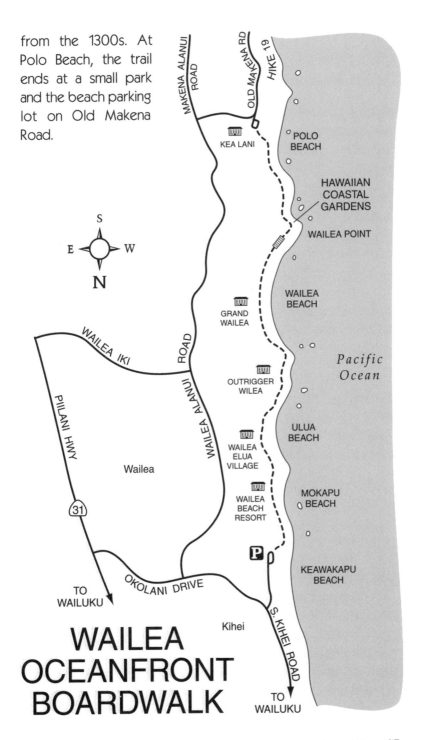

WAILEA OCEANFRONT BOARDWALK

Hike 19
Palauea Beach
to Haloa Point and Poolenalena Beach

Hiking distance: 2 miles round trip
Hiking time: 1 hour
Elevation gain: 20 feet
Maps: U.S.G.S. Makena
       Island Of Maui Recreation Map

Summary of hike: Palauea Beach is a beautiful, undeveloped white sand beach backed by a forest of kiawe. The beach is bordered to the north by Polo Beach and to the south by Haloa Point. The wide promontory has an ancient Hawaiian fisherman's shrine (heiau) overlooking the ocean. From the stone-enclosed heiau, the footpath descends into Poolenalena Beach, a wide, half-mile long, undeveloped white sand beach. The beach is divided by several rocky lava points.

Driving directions: At the south end of Kihei, the South Kihei Road ends. The road curves left at the signed entrance to Wailea on Okolani Drive. Go one block to the junction with Wailea Alanui Road on the right. Turn right and drive 1.7 miles south to Kaukahi Street, just past the Kea Lani Hotel. Turn right and go 0.2 miles to Old Makena Road. On the right is the parking lot for Polo Beach (Hike 18). Turn left and drive 0.2 miles to Palauea Beach. Park on either side of the road.

Hiking directions: Walk through one of the many openings in the fence, entering the shady kiawe grove behind the sandy beach. Bear left, heading south on the beach strand or through the forested paths along the back side of the beach. Various interconnecting paths climb onto Haloa Point, requiring some rock scrambling. Pass Koa, an ancient Hawaiian fishing shrine overlooking the ocean. Continue to the sands of Poolenalena Beach. Follow the isolated beach strand, choosing you own turnaround spot. The trail ends at the rocky point at the south end of the beach.

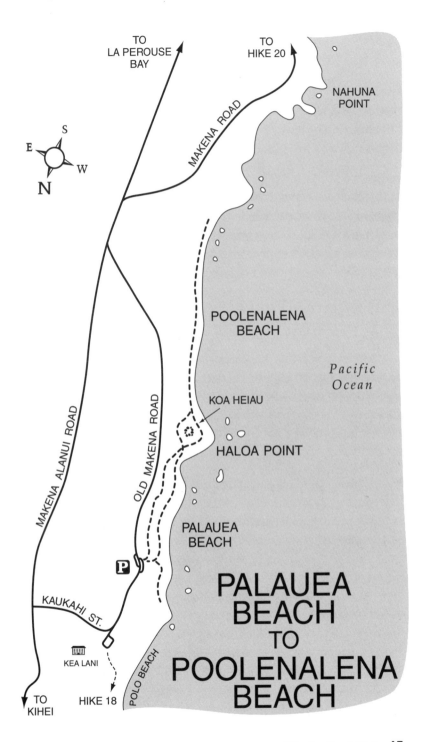

TO
LA PEROUSE
BAY

TO
HIKE 20

NAHUNA
POINT

MAKENA ROAD

S
E · W
N

POOLENALENA
BEACH

*Pacific
Ocean*

KOA HEIAU

OLD MAKENA ROAD

MAKENA ALANUI ROAD

HALOA POINT

PALAUEA
BEACH

P

KAUKAHI ST.

KEA LANI

TO
KIHEI

HIKE 18

POLO BEACH

PALAUEA
BEACH
TO
POOLENALENA
BEACH

Hike 20
Maluaka Beach

Hiking distance: 1.2 miles round trip
Hiking time: 40 minutes
Elevation gain: Level
Maps: U.S.G.S. Makena
  Island Of Maui Recreation Map

Summary of hike: Maluaka Beach is a small sandy beach in Makena Bay bordered to the north by Keawalai Point. The beach is adjacent to Keawalai Church, founded in 1832, and the historic graveyard. The protected beach cove is backed by sand dunes and kiawe trees. On the grassy bluffs to the south is a landscaped park, picnic area and the Maui Prince Hotel. The low rocky bluffs of Maluaka Point separate the beach from the black sand of Oneuli Beach. From the bluffs are gorgeous views of the coastline.

Driving directions: At the south end of Kihei, the South Kihei Road ends. The road curves left at the signed entrance to Wailea on Okolani Drive. Go one block to the junction with Wailea Alanui Road on the right. Turn right and drive 3 miles south to Makena Road. (Wailea Alanui Road becomes Makena Alanui Road along the way.) Turn right and continue 0.8 miles to the parking lot on the left, across the road from the historic Keawalai Church.

A second parking lot is is at the south end of the beach near Maluaka Point. Access is on an unmarked turnoff from Makena Alanui Road, shortly after passing the Maui Prince Hotel.

Hiking directions: From the Makena Road parking lot, walk a short distance south on the road to the Maluaka Beach access near the end of the road. Follow the tree-lined crescent of sand to the south end of the bay. Climb up the grassy bluffs by the Maui Prince Hotel. Steps lead up to the grassy knoll and picnic area landscaped with trees. Cross the knoll southwest towards Maluaka Point. Hop over the low lava rock wall, and skirt the edge of the golf course along the cliff's edge. Views extend south across the beautiful bay to Puu Olai (Hike 21). From the grassy bluffs, a path heads inland through the picnic area to the second parking lot. Return along the same paths.

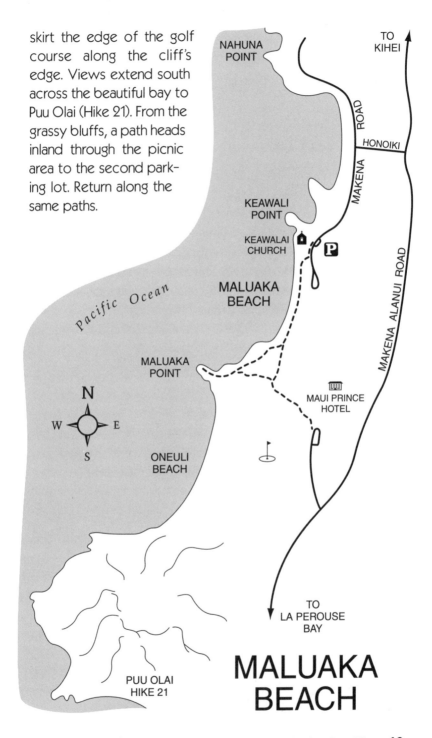

NAHUNA POINT

TO KIHEI

MAKENA ROAD

HONOIKI

MAKENA ALANUI ROAD

KEAWALI POINT

KEAWALAI CHURCH

P

MALUAKA BEACH

Pacific Ocean

MALUAKA POINT

MAUI PRINCE HOTEL

N
W E
S

ONEULI BEACH

TO LA PEROUSE BAY

PUU OLAI HIKE 21

MALUAKA BEACH

Hike 21
Puu Olai "Red Hill"
from Oneloa "Makena" Beach

Hiking distance: 1 mile round trip
Hiking time: 1 hour
Elevation gain: 400 feet
Maps: U.S.G.S. Makena

Summary of hike: Puu Olai is a 360-foot weathered volcanic tuft that protrudes out to sea at the south end of Wailea. The dormant cinder cone separates Oneloa "Makena" Beach from Oneuli "Black Sand" Beach. At the base of the Puu Olai are lava formations and tidepools, dividing Makena Beach into Big Beach and Little Beach (an unofficial clothing optional beach). This hike begins on Big Beach and follows the long and wide crescent of sand to the base of the cinder cone. The trail explores the tidepools fronting Puu Olai, then climbs the volcanic slope to panoramic views across the ocean to the islands of Lanai, Molokini and Kahoolawe.

Driving directions: At the south end of Kihei, the South Kihei Road ends. The road curves left at the signed entrance to Wailea on Okolani Drive. Go one block to the junction with Wailea Alanui Road on the right. Turn right and drive 4.8 miles south to the signed Makena State Beach turnoff. (Wailea Alanui Road becomes Makena Alanui Road along the way.) Turn right on the entrance road, and park in the lot a short distance ahead.

Hiking directions: Walk out to the wide crescent of white sand along Big Beach. Follow the wide strand to the right. Head about 200 yards northwest to the base of Puu Olai, the hill separating Big Beach from Little Beach. Climb up the low lava wall to the ridge overlooking the two beaches. Begin ascending the steep trail to the right on the southern slope of Puu Olai. There are magnificent vistas at the summit. After savoring the views, return to the base of the hill, and venture out on the lava point, where tidepools abound. Explore along your own route.

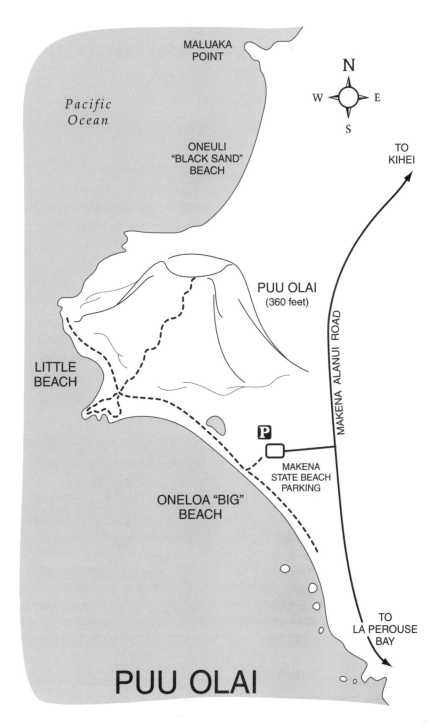

MALUAKA POINT

Pacific Ocean

ONEULI "BLACK SAND" BEACH

N
W   E
S

TO KIHEI

PUU OLAI
(360 feet)

MAKENA ALANUI ROAD

LITTLE BEACH

P

MAKENA STATE BEACH PARKING

ONELOA "BIG" BEACH

TO LA PEROUSE BAY

PUU OLAI

Hike 22
Ahihi-Kinau Natural Area Reserve
Northern Trail

Hiking distance: 1.4 miles round trip
Hiking time: 1 hour
Elevation gain: Level
Maps: U.S.G.S. Makena
  Island Of Maui Recreation Map

map next page

Summary of hike: The Ahihi-Kinau Natural Area Reserve on Cape Kinau is a 2,045-acre barren land mass that is covered in black lava. The lava is from a flow down the southwest slope of Haleakala in 1790, the last active flow on Maui. The surreal, desolate landscape is blanketed with loose, jagged aa lava. It is bordered by Ahihi Bay to the north and La Perouse Bay to the south. The road from Makena to La Perouse Bay crosses through the reserve, passing several trail access points. The trails across the stark moonscape lead to kiawe groves, inland ponds, tide-pools and boulder-lined beaches. Views extend beyond the Puu Olai crater to the West Maui Mountains and to the islands of Kahoolawe and Molokini.

Driving directions: At the south end of Kihei, the South Kihei Road ends. The road curves left at the signed entrance to Wailea on Okolani Drive. Go one block to the junction with Wailea Alanui Road on the right. Turn right and drive 6.3 miles south to the large trailhead parking area on the right. (Wailea Alanui Road becomes Makena Alanui Road along the way.)

Hiking directions: Take the signed path into the massive, exposed lava field, crossing the north end of Cape Kinau. The path reaches the rocky beach at 0.2 miles. Follow the jagged coastline south past endless inlets and tidepools. Ka Lae Mamane, the northwest point, is at 0.7 miles. This is our turn-around spot.

To hike further, explore along your own route, as both inland and coastline trails cross this natural preserve.

Hike 23
Ahihi-Kinau Natural Area Reserve
Southern Trail

Hiking distance: 1.6 miles round trip
Hiking time: 1 hour
Elevation gain: 50 feet
Maps: U.S.G.S. Makena

map
next page

Summary of hike: Cape Kinau is an enormous land mass formed by a 1790 lava flow from the southwest slopes of Haleakala. The desolate area has been preserved as the Ahihi-Kinau Natural Area Reserve. The surreal landscape is covered in fields of rough, unstable black lava rock with inland ponds. The coastline has boulder-lined beaches with endless tidepools. The Southern Trail leads through kiawe forests to the shores of La Perouse Bay. The stunning cobalt blue waters in the bay are as clear and rich as the mind can imagine. The snorkeling here is among the best on the island.

Driving directions: At the south end of Kihei, the South Kihei Road ends. The road curves left at the signed entrance to Wailea on Okolani Drive. Go one block to the junction with Wailea Alanui Road on the right. Turn right and drive 7.6 miles south to the parking pullout on the left, across the road from the signed trailhead on the right. (Wailea Alanui Road becomes Makena Alanui Road along the way.)

Hiking directions: Walk past the trail sign at the lava rock wall, entering a kiawe forest. Follow the fenceline on the left. Cross a sandy area, emerging from the forest to the exposed lava field where the coastal views are excellent. Descend to the shoreline of La Perouse Bay. From the hill along the north end of the bay, climb up to fantastic views across the bay. Continue following the jagged shoreline to numerous inlets that are perfect for snorkeling. The trail reaches Kalaeloa Point at 0.8 miles on the west side of La Perouse Bay. The area has exceptional water pockets to explore. Choose your own turnaround spot.

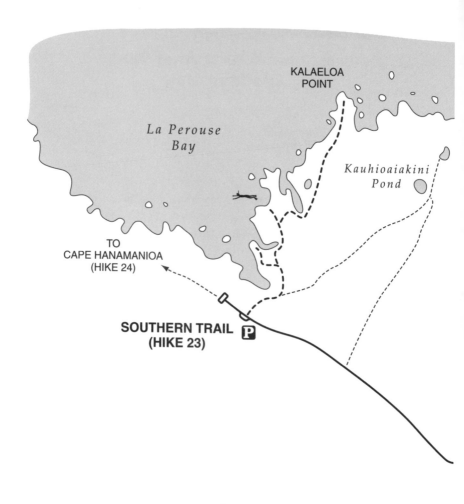

KALAELOA
POINT

*La Perouse
Bay*

*Kauhioaiakini
Pond*

TO
CAPE HANAMANIOA
(HIKE 24)

SOUTHERN TRAIL
(HIKE 23)

S
W
E
N

AHINI–KINAU
NATURAL AREA RESERVE
HIKES 22–23

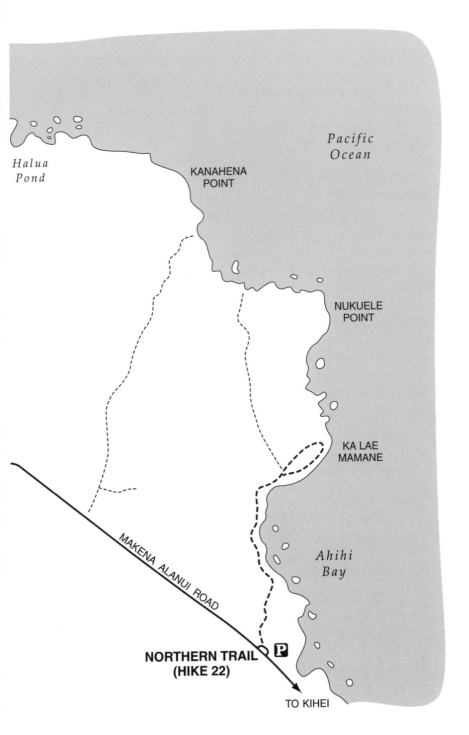

Halua Pond

Pacific Ocean

KANAHENA POINT

NUKUELE POINT

KA LAE MAMANE

MAKENA ALANUI ROAD

Ahihi Bay

NORTHERN TRAIL (HIKE 22)

🅿

TO KIHEI

Hike 24
La Perouse Bay to Cape Hanamanioa

Hiking distance: 3 miles round trip
Hiking time: 1.5 hours
Elevation gain: 50 feet
Maps: U.S.G.S. Makena

Summary of hike: This hike begins at La Perouse Bay, an isolated bay at the southwest tip of Maui. The trail passes tidepools, rocky coves, lava formations, ancient rock walls and enclosures to a light beacon on the tip of Cape Hanamanioa. The oceans surrounds the beacon on three sides while Haleakala towers above to the northeast. The hike skirts La Perouse Bay along a rutted jeep road that runs parallel to the "King's Highway." The "King's Highway," an ancient Hoapili Trail, was constructed with rough lava rock between 1824–1840.

Driving directions: At the south end of Kihei, the South Kihei Road ends. The road curves left at the signed entrance to Wailea on Okolani Drive. Go one block to the junction with Wailea Alanui Road on the right. Turn right and drive 7.8 miles south, passing Wailea and Makena, to the end of the paved road. The signed parking area is on the left side of the road. (Wailea Alanui Road becomes Makena Alanui Road.)

Hiking directions: Head south on the unpaved road, parallel to the ocean. The road joins the shoreline and curves around La Perouse Bay. Under the shade of kiave trees, pass tidepools and lava formations. At 0.5 miles, just beyond Beau Chien Beach, the sandy, shaded trail crosses a stark lava field. On the right is an ancient square lava rock enclosure. On the left, at the fenceline, is an signed connector path to the Hoapili "King's Highway" Trail. Continue on the jeep road, passing a second connector trail with the Hoapili Trail at one mile. Follow the rutted road up the hill onto Cape Hanamanioa to a saddle overlooking La Perouse Bay. The extensive lava flow on the slope of Haleakala can be seen from here. The loose, rocky trail makes walking difficult. Continue 0.3 miles to the southwest point of Cape Hanamanioa at the light beacon surrounded by ocean. Narrow side paths lead to several overlooks; fisherman trails follow the low sea cliffs. Return by taking the same path back.

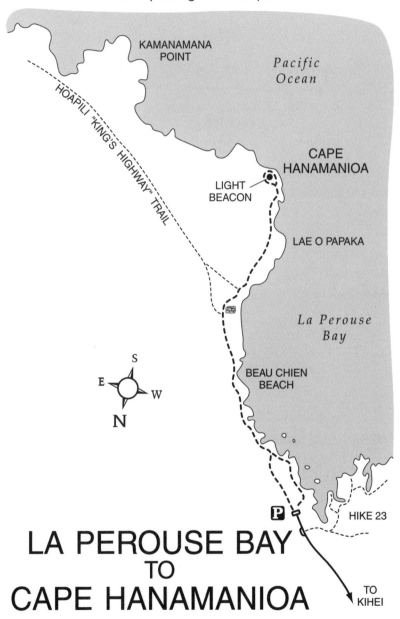

KAMANAMANA
POINT

*Pacific
Ocean*

HOAPILI "KING'S" HIGHWAY" TRAIL

CAPE
HANAMANIOA

LIGHT
BEACON

LAE O PAPAKA

*La Perouse
Bay*

S

E ⊕ W

N

BEAU CHIEN
BEACH

P

HIKE 23

LA PEROUSE BAY
TO
CAPE HANAMANIOA

TO
KIHEI

Hike 25
Kanaha Pond Wildlife Sanctuary

Permit needed from the Department of Natural Resources
54 S. High Street, Suite 101, Wailuku (808) 984-8100
Sanctuary is open to the public October—March
Observation shelter is open year around

Hiking distance: 1.5 miles round trip
Hiking time: 1 hour
Elevation gain: Level
Maps: U.S.G.S. Paia and Wailuku
  Island of Maui Recreation Map

Summary of hike: Kanaha Pond Wildlife Sanctuary is a 143-acre preserve and nesting site for endangered and migratory birds. Looping paths circle the perimeter of the wetland sanctuary through a shaded forest with native plants. There are numerous abandoned concrete World War II bunkers along the trails. The wildlife sanctuary is adjacent to the town of Kahului.

Driving directions: From Wailuku, drive 2.5 miles east on Highway 32, bearing to the right onto Highway 36 (Hana Highway). Continue for one block and turn left onto Highway 396. The Kanaha Pond Observation Shelter and parking lot is on the left a half block ahead. To enter the sanctuary trails, drive another block to Dairy Road and turn left. Continue one more block to Palipali Road. Turn left and park in the lot.

Hiking directions: Walk through the entrance gate and follow the unpaved service road/trail over the canal. Continue straight ahead along the fenceline to the north end of the sanctuary, near Kanaha Beach Park (Hike 26). Bear left, winding through the shaded trail. Wander around, choosing your own route. Only one road completes a loop back to the trailhead.

For the short walk to the observation shelter off Highway 396, go through the entrance gate, and follow the 100-yard walkway on the peninsula to the viewing kiosk over the pond.

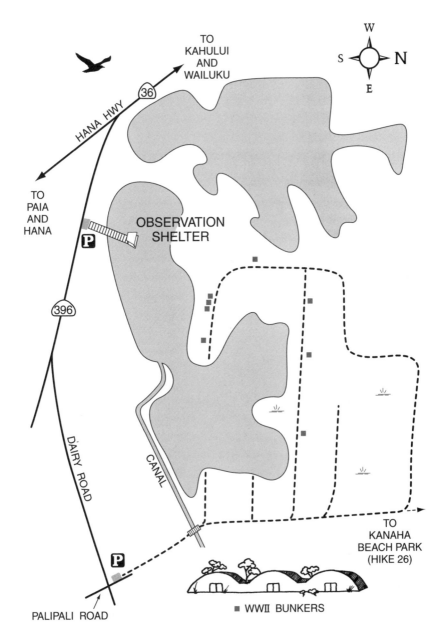

KANAHA POND
WILDLIFE SANCTUARY

Hike 26
Kanaha Beach Park

Hiking distance: 2.4 miles round trip
Hiking time: 1.5 hours
Elevation gain: Level
Maps: U.S.G.S. Paia and Wailuku
Island of Maui Recreation Map

Summary of hike: Kanaha Beach Park, adjacent to the Kahului airport, is a tree-lined park backed by a large, grassy, shady picnic area. A mile long strip of white sand lies between the grassy area and the ocean. Kanaha Beach is divided into a series of smaller pockets by rock jetties that help slow down erosion. At the west end of the beach is Hobron Point, bordering the Kahului Harbor. The steady trade winds that sweep across the Maui isthmus make this an excellent and popular windsurfing beach.

Driving directions: From Highway 32 (Kaahumanu Avenue) in Kahului, near the airport, turn left on 32A. Drive one block and curve right on Amala Place. Continue 1.7 miles to the second Kanaha Beach Park entrance on the left. Turn left and park in the lot a short distance ahead.

Hiking directions: Walk towards the beach, crossing the large grassy picnic area through a shady kiawe tree grove. Near the shoreline, head west (left). Stroll through the tree grove or follow the sandy beach parallel to the coastline. The trails cross rolling dunes and offer great views of the West Maui Mountains. At about one mile, shortly before reaching Hobron Point and the harbor, the area becomes industrial with oil tanks and buildings. This is a good turnaround spot.

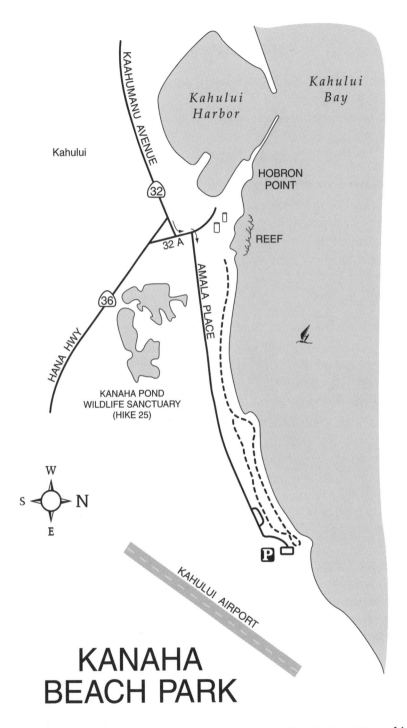

KAAHUMANU AVENUE

Kahului

32

32 A

36

HANA HWY

AMALA PLACE

*Kahului
Harbor*

*Kahului
Bay*

HOBRON
POINT

REEF

KANAHA POND
WILDLIFE SANCTUARY
(HIKE 25)

W
N
S
E

P

KAHULUI AIRPORT

KANAHA
BEACH PARK

Hike 27
Spreckelsville Beach

Hiking distance: 2 miles round trip
Hiking time: 1 hour
Elevation gain: Level
Maps: U.S.G.S. Paia
      Island of Maui Recreation Map

Summary of hike: Spreckelsville Beach is a wide, uncrowded white sand beach in a sweeping bay with numerous rocky points. The community of Spreckelsville backs the beach, which is isolated by large sand dunes covered with naupaka plants. The beach is a popular windsurfing location that is bordered on the west by Papaula Point, separating it from Kanaha Beach Park (Hike 26). To the east is Baldwin Beach Park (Hike 28).

Driving directions: From Kahului, take the Hana Highway (36) east to the junction with the Haleakala Highway (37). Continue 1.4 miles east on the Hana Highway (36) to the unmarked Spreckelsville Beach Road, a paved road on the left. Turn left and drive about a half mile. Turn right on any of the several dirt roads on the right. They all lead to the sandy beachfront near the west end of the beach.

Another access is available on the east end of the beach. From the Spreckelsville Beach Road turnoff, drive 0.7 miles east on the Hana Highway and turn left on Nonohe Street, just past mile marker 4. At a quarter mile turn left again on Kealakai Place. Park at the end of the road near the oceanfront.

Hiking directions: From Papaula Point, cross the open expanse of sand dunes to the isolated shoreline near the point. To the left (west) the trail curves around Papaula Point and past residences, reaching Kanaha Beach Park. To the right (east), stroll across the wide beach and rolling dunes. Along the way, pass several rocky points, the community of Spreckelsville and the Maui Country Club. Beyond Wawau Point, the beach connects with Baldwin Beach Park. Choose your own turnaround spot.

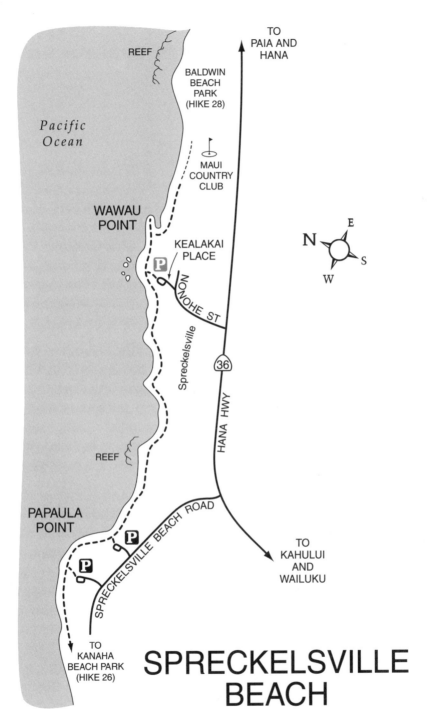

REEF

Pacific Ocean

TO
PAIA AND
HANA

BALDWIN
BEACH
PARK
(HIKE 28)

MAUI
COUNTRY
CLUB

WAWAU
POINT

KEALAKAI
PLACE

N E
W S

Spreckelsville

NONOHE ST

36

HANA HWY

REEF

PAPAULA
POINT

SPRECKELSVILLE BEACH ROAD

TO
KAHULUI
AND
WAILUKU

TO
KANAHA
BEACH PARK
(HIKE 26)

SPRECKELSVILLE BEACH

Hike 28
H. A. Baldwin Beach Park

Hiking distance: 2 miles round trip
Hiking time: 1 hour
Elevation gain: Level
Maps: U.S.G.S. Paia
Island of Maui Recreation Map

Summary of hike: H. A. Baldwin Park is a picturesque park that was originally developed as a private recreation area for the Hawaiian Sugar Company employees. It became a public beach park in 1963. The park has a large grassy picnic area with tables, grills, a pavilion and a protected swimming cove. A white sand beach fronts the park. On the east end is an ironwood and palm tree grove and a low rocky bluff. The park lies between Paia Bay and Spreckelsville Beach Park (Hike 27).

Driving directions: From the junction of the Hana Highway (36) and the Haleakala Highway (37) near the airport, drive 5.1 miles on the Hana Highway to the signed H. A. Baldwin Beach Park turnoff on the left by mile marker 6. Turn left and drive 0.2 miles to the parking area at the beachfront.
From Baldwin Avenue in Paia, the turnoff is 0.8 miles west.

Hiking directions: Walk across the grassy picnic area towards the beach. Take the path to the east (right) following either the sandy shoreline or the grassy knoll. Follow the coastline through a kiawe and ironwood tree grove, crossing the low rocky bluff. A wide path parallels the coastline on the rocky bluff into Lower Paia Park at 0.6 miles.
Return to the grassy picnic area of Baldwin Park and head west (left). Beachcomb along the white sand crescent to Wawau Point, a rocky point with a protected swimming area.

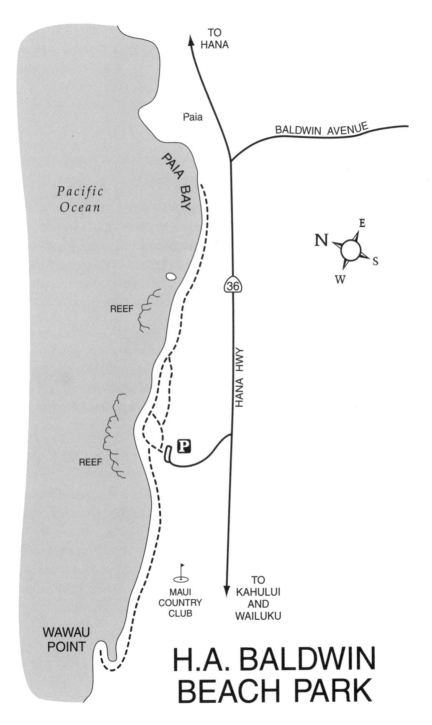

TO
HANA

Paia

BALDWIN AVENUE

PAIA BAY

*Pacific
Ocean*

REEF

N
E
S
W

(36)

HANA HWY

REEF

P

MAUI
COUNTRY
CLUB

TO
KAHULUI
AND
WAILUKU

WAWAU
POINT

H.A. BALDWIN
BEACH PARK

Hike 29
Hookipa Beach Park

Hiking distance: 1 mile round trip
Hiking time: 30 minutes
Elevation gain: 80 feet
Maps: U.S.G.S. Paia
      Island of Maui Recreation Map

Summary of hike: Hookipa Beach Park sits alongside the Hana Highway a short distance east of Paia. The park is in a beautiful cliff-lined bay that is spread between two lava rock points and backed by a rocky shelf. The beach is best known as the premier windsurfing beach on Maui and, arguably, in the world. The bay plays host to the world's top windsurfers. The trail leads down the bluffs to a small rocky beach with tidepools and natural arches. It is fascinating to watch the windsurfers at Hookipa from the observation overlook at the elevated parking area atop the cliffs.

Driving directions: From the junction of Highway 36 (Hana Highway) and Baldwin Avenue in downtown Paia, take the Hana Highway 2.2 miles to the Hookipa Lookout parking lot on the left, between mile markers 8 and 9.

Hiking directions: From the overlook, follow the cliff's edge to the right (northeast), and descend to the oceanfront lava bed. Explore the various tidepools and rock formations at the point. Curve to the left along the coastal cliffs, reaching the sandy beach. Cross the beach to the footpath at the base of the hillside at the west end. Walk up the grassy bluffs to vistas of the bay. Return parallel to the parking lot road overlooking the bay.

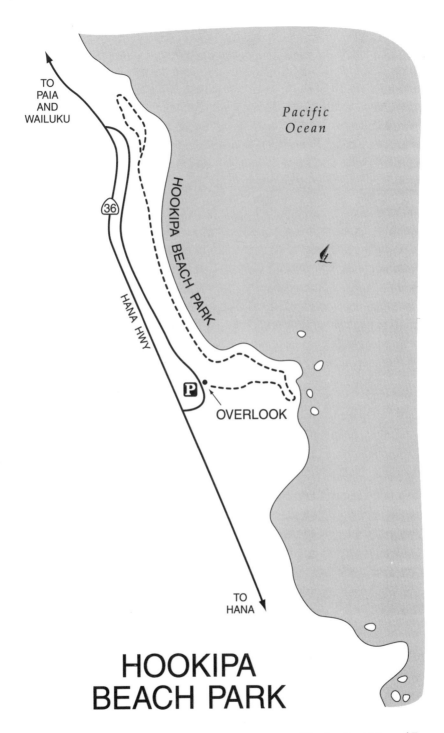

TO
PAIA
AND
WAILUKU

*Pacific
Ocean*

36

HANA HWY

HOOKIPA BEACH PARK

P

OVERLOOK

TO
HANA

HOOKIPA
BEACH PARK

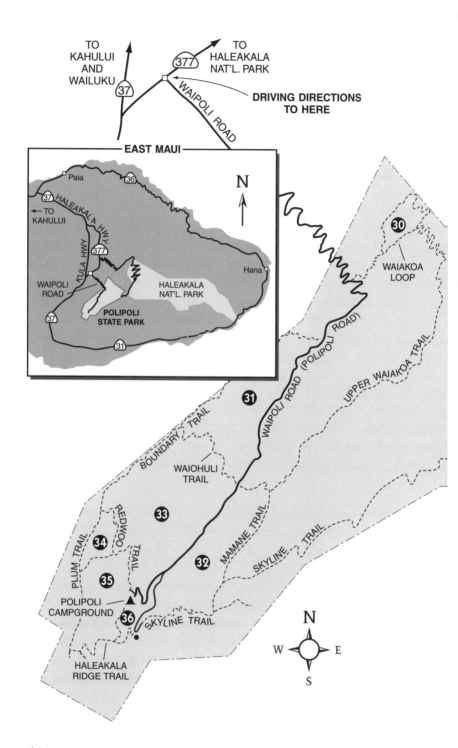

TO
KAHULUI
AND
WAILUKU
37

TO
HALEAKALA
NAT'L. PARK
377

WAIPOLI ROAD

DRIVING DIRECTIONS TO HERE

EAST MAUI

N

Paia
36
37 HALEAKALA HWY
←TO
KAHULUI
377
KULA HWY
WAIPOLI
ROAD
37
Hana
HALEAKALA
NAT'L. PARK
**POLIPOLI
STATE PARK**
31

WAIAKOA
LOOP
30

WAIPOLI ROAD (POLIPOLI ROAD)

UPPER WAIAKOA TRAIL

N

31

BOUNDARY TRAIL

WAIOHULI
TRAIL

33

MAMANE TRAIL

SKYLINE TRAIL

32

PLUM TRAIL

REDWOOD TRAIL

34

35

POLIPOLI
CAMPGROUND

36

SKYLINE TRAIL

HALEAKALA
RIDGE TRAIL

N
W · E
S

POLIPOLI STATE PARK
KULA FOREST RESERVE
HIKES 30-36

Polipoli State Park, at 6,200 feet, is part of the 12,000-acre Kula Forest Reserve on the upper southern and western slopes of Haleakala. An extensive trail system crisscrosses the highland forest reserve and connects to the summit of Haleakala. Well-marked trails weave through a profusion of giant redwoods, Monterey cypress, sugi pine, cedar, eucalyptus, plum, alder and ash groves introduced in the 1920s and 1930s. The quiet, exotic, cloud-shrouded forest, with an understory of ferns and mosses, is reminiscent of the Pacific Northwest. The paths lead to old ranger stations, Civilian Conservation Corps (CCC) bunkhouses, cinder cones, caves and a campground. Panoramic views extend across Central and West Maui, including the islands of Lanai, Molokai and Kahoolawe.

The weather is frequently damp and cool due to the high altitude. Wear appropriate clothing.

TO
HALEAKALA
NAT'L. PARK

Driving directions to Waipoli Road:

From Kahului, near the airport, head east on the Hana Highway (36), and turn right on the Haleakala Highway (37). Drive 14 miles upcountry, passing Pukalani, to the second signed junction with 377, just before mile marker 14. (Highway 37 becomes the Kula Highway after Pukalani.) Turn left onto 377 (Kekaulike Avenue). Continue 0.4 miles to Waipoli Road and turn right.

Continue down Waipoli Road in accordance with each hike's directions.

Hike 30
Waiakoa Loop Trail

Hiking distance: 4.5 miles round trip
Hiking time: 2 hours
Elevation gain: 600 feet
Maps: U.S.G.S. Kilohana
      Recreational Trails of the Kula Forest Reserve

Summary of hike: The Waiakoa Loop is a 3-mile loop trail in the Kula Forest Reserve on the slopes of Haleakala. The hike contours the hillside with panoramic views down country and across open grasslands. Switchbacks then descend 500 feet into a draw, winding through forested groves of eucalyptus and pines. The hike connects with the trail system inside Polipoli State Park.

Driving direction: Follow the driving directions on page 68 to Waipoli Road. From Waipoli Road, continue 5 miles up this steep winding road to the signed Waiakoa Trail on the left by the green hunter check-in station. Park on the left off the road.

Hiking directions: Head north past the hunter station on the dirt road overlooking the valley. Cross Kaonoulu Gulch and enter a eucalyptus forest, reaching the Kula Forest Reserve trailhead sign and gate at 0.75 miles. A short distance past the gate is a trail split and the start of the loop. Take the footpath uphill to the right and cross Naalae Gulch. Emerge from the trees to fantastic views on the open rolling grasslands. The path reaches a signed junction with the Upper Waiakoa Trail at 1.3 miles. This route bears to the right, connecting with the Mamane and Waihuli Trails (Hike 32). Continue straight, traversing the hillside and crossing Keahuaiwi Gulch. Curve left, descending 500 feet on five switchbacks into the shaded pine forest. Curve left again and return to the south. Switchbacks steadily wind back up the hillside, completing the loop. Bear to the right, retracing your steps to the parking area.

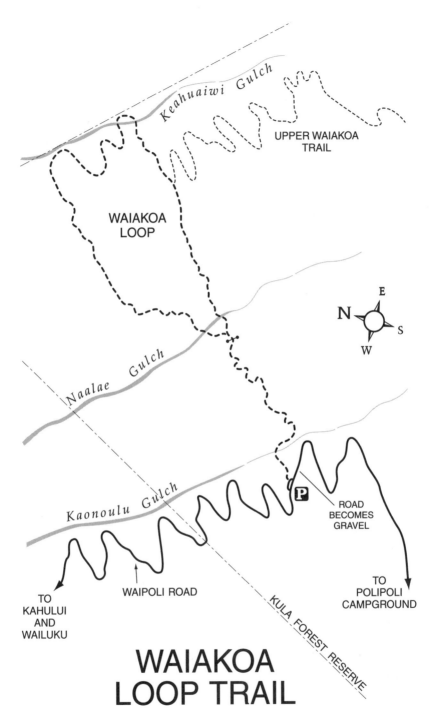

Keahuaiwi Gulch

UPPER WAIAKOA
TRAIL

WAIAKOA
LOOP

N E S W

Naalae Gulch

Kaonoulu Gulch

P

ROAD
BECOMES
GRAVEL

TO
KAHULUI
AND
WAILUKU

WAIPOLI ROAD

KULA FOREST RESERVE

TO
POLIPOLI
CAMPGROUND

WAIAKOA
LOOP TRAIL

Hike 31
Boundary-Waiohuli Loop
Polipoli State Park

Hiking distance: 5.8 mile loop
Hiking time: 3 hours
Elevation gain: 850 feet
Maps: U.S.G.S. Kilohana and Lualailua Hills
Recreation Trails of the Kula Forest Reserve

Summary of hike: The Boundary-Waiohuli Loop winds through the shade of a towering forest with a lush understory of vegetation. The forested path descends along the north Kula Forest Reserve boundary, then follows the west boundary to an old cabin at the junction with the Waiohuli Trail. The Waiohuli Trail climbs 800 feet, passing through dense stands of redwood, cedar and ash trees.

Driving directions: Follow the driving directions on page 68 to Waipoli Road. From Waipoli Road, continue 5.9 miles up this steep winding road to the end of the pavement. Follow the unpaved road a half mile to the signed Boundary Trail on the right. Park on the side of the road.

Hiking directions: Take the Boundary Trail and immediately descend into the dense forest to the west. The path weaves a half mile downhill to the northwest boundary of the Kula Forest Reserve. Curve south, skirting the west boundary through the deep forest. Cross numerous small gulches. At 2.6 miles, the trail reaches a signed junction by a rustic shelter on the left. The right fork continues on the Boundary Trail towards the old ranger station at the Redwood Trail junction (Hike 33). Leave the Boundary Trail, and take the Waiohuli Trail to the left. Steadily climb through the dense forest, reaching the Waipoli Road at 4 miles. Follow the forested access road to the left for 1.8 miles, completing the loop at the trailhead.

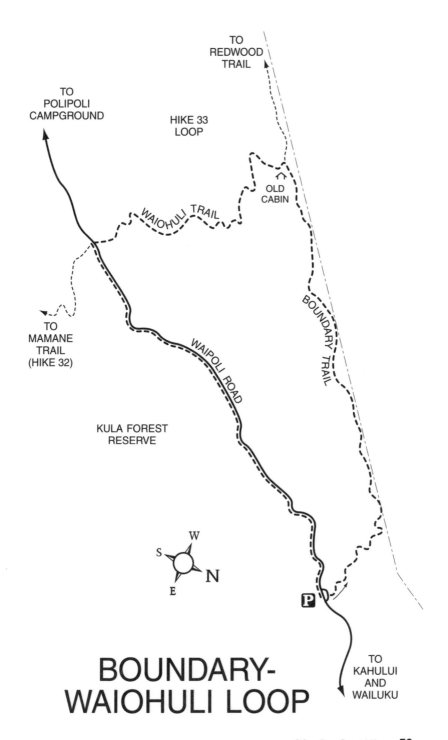

TO
REDWOOD
TRAIL

TO
POLIPOLI
CAMPGROUND

HIKE 33
LOOP

WAIOHULI TRAIL

OLD
CABIN

TO
MAMANE
TRAIL
(HIKE 32)

WAIPOLI ROAD

BOUNDARY TRAIL

KULA FOREST
RESERVE

W
S   N
E

P

TO
KAHULUI
AND
WAILUKU

BOUNDARY-
WAIOHULI LOOP

Hike 32
Mamane-Skyline Loop
Polipoli State Park

Hiking distance: 4 mile loop
Hiking time: 2 hours
Elevation gain: 850 feet
Maps: U.S.G.S. Lualailua Hills and Makena
       Recreation Trails of the Kula Forest Reserve

Summary of hike: The Mamane Trail leads to a small volcanic cone and cave shelter before joining the Skyline Trail at 7,300 feet. The Skyline Trail is a dirt road that follows the ridge along the southwest slope of Haleakala all the way to Science City Road near the Haleakala summit. This hike follows the lower portion of the trail, looping back through Polipoli State Park.

Driving directions: Follow the driving directions on page 68 to Waipoli Road. From Waipoli Road, continue 5.9 miles up this steep winding road to the end of the pavement. Follow the unpaved road 2.3 miles to the signed Waiohuli Trail on both sides of the road. Park on the side of the road.

Hiking directions: Take the signed Waiohuli Trail on the left (east) side of the road, heading uphill. Zigzag up the mountain through a pine forest, reaching a signed junction at 0.7 miles. The left fork leads to the Waiakoa Loop Trail (Hike 30) on the Upper Waiakoa Loop. Take the right fork on the Mamane Trail. There are caves and a lava pit crater on the right. Wind steadily up the mountain, reaching Skyline Trail, an unpaved road, at 1.9 miles. Bear to the right on the dirt road, and descend along the exposed slope through a eucalyptus grove for a half mile to a trail junction. Again bear right, winding down the mountain to a sharp hairpin bend in the road. On the bend is an overlook and a junction with the Haleakala Ridge Trail (Hike 36). Follow the road downhill, passing the junction with the campground road on the left. Continue straight ahead on the Waipoli Road one mile, completing the loop back at the trailhead.

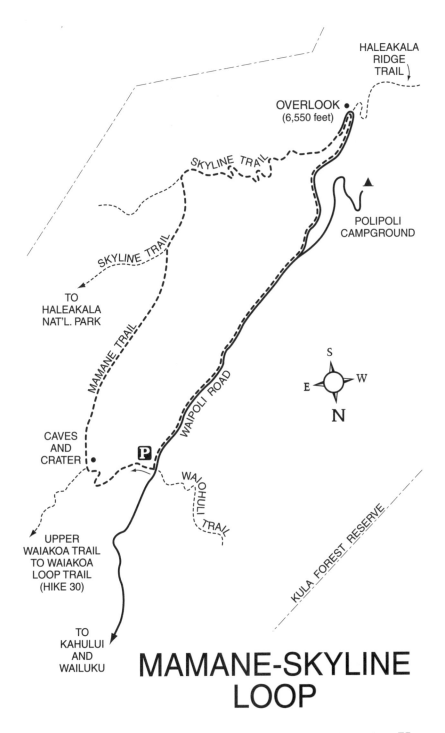

HALEAKALA
RIDGE
TRAIL

OVERLOOK
(6,550 feet)

SKYLINE TRAIL

POLIPOLI
CAMPGROUND

SKYLINE TRAIL

TO
HALEAKALA
NAT'L. PARK

MAMANE TRAIL

WAIPOLI ROAD

S

E ⬥ W

N

CAVES
AND
CRATER

P

WAIOHULI TRAIL

UPPER
WAIAKOA TRAIL
TO WAIAKOA
LOOP TRAIL
(HIKE 30)

KULA FOREST RESERVE

TO
KAHULUI
AND
WAILUKU

MAMANE-SKYLINE LOOP

Hike 33
Redwood-Boundary-Waiohuli Loop
Polipoli State Park

Hiking distance: 6.1 mile loop
Hiking time: 3 hours
Elevation gain: 1,000 feet
Maps: U.S.G.S. Lualailua Hills and Makena
Recreation Trails of the Kula Forest Reserve

Summary of hike: The Redwood Trail descends from the Polipoli Campground through a mature forest of giant redwoods, cedars, pines and ash. The atmospheric path, frequently shrouded in a foggy mist, connects with the Boundary Trail at an old ranger station and a huge hydrangea garden. The Boundary Trail then follows the west boundary to an old cabin shelter at the junction with the Waiohuli Trail. The Waiohuli Trail winds up the hillside to the Waipoli Road through dense stands of redwood, cedar and ash trees.

Driving directions: Follow the driving directions on page 68 to Waipoli Road. From Waipoli Road, continue 5.9 miles up this steep winding road to the end of the pavement. Follow the unpaved road 3.3 miles to a road split. Take the right fork 0.6 miles, descending to the campground and parking area at the end of the road.

Hiking directions: Walk 50 yards back up the entrance road to the signed Redwood Trail on the left by the yellow gate. Walk through the gate and down the road to a camping cabin. The signed footpath is on the right, just before reaching the cabin. Descend through the dense forest to a signed junction with the Tie Trail at 0.8 miles. Stay on the Redwood Trail to the right, and continue downhill past an old CCC bunkhouse on the left. A short distance ahead is a signed 3-way junction at 1.7 miles. The left fork passes the old ranger station on the Plum Trail (Hike 34). Take the right fork and head north on the Boundary Trail. Skirt the west boundary of the Kula Forest

Reserve to a cabin and signed junction in the deep forest at 3.1 miles. The left fork continues on the Boundary Trail (Hike 31). Go to the right on the Waiohuli Trail, steadily winding uphill through the lush forest to Waipoli Road at 4.5 miles. Bear right, following the road one mile to the road split. Take the right fork back to the campground and parking area.

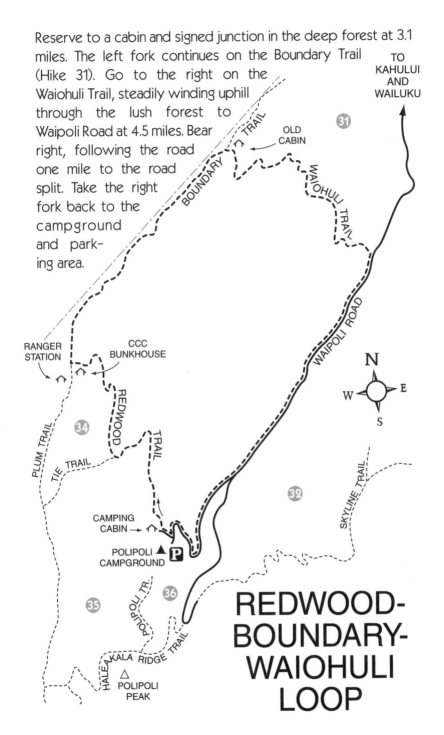

TO KAHULUI AND WAILUKU

OLD CABIN

BOUNDARY TRAIL

WAIOHULI TRAIL

31

RANGER STATION

CCC BUNKHOUSE

REDWOOD TRAIL

WAIPOLI ROAD

34

PLUM TRAIL

TIE TRAIL

N
W   E
S

CAMPING CABIN

POLIPOLI CAMPGROUND

P

32

SKYLINE TRAIL

35

POLIPOLI TR.

36

HALEAKALA RIDGE TRAIL

POLIPOLI PEAK

REDWOOD-
BOUNDARY-
WAIOHULI
LOOP

Hike 34
Redwood-Plum-Tie Loop
Polipoli State Park

Hiking distance: 4 miles round trip
Hiking time: 2 hours
Elevation gain: 900 feet
Maps: U.S.G.S. Lualailua Hills and Makena
  Recreation Trails of the Kula Forest Reserve

Summary of hike: The Redwood Trail begins near the Polipoli Campground at 6,200 feet. The trail descends through magnificent stands of towering redwoods mixed with cedars, pines and ash. At the bottom is a three-way junction with the Plum and Boundary Trails, a Civilian Conservation Corps bunkhouse, an old ranger station and a massive wall of flowering hydrangea bushes. The hike returns on the Tie Trail, a connector route between the Redwood and Plum Trails.

Driving directions: Follow the driving directions on page 68 to Waipoli Road. From Waipoli Road, continue 5.9 miles up this steep winding road to the end of the pavement. Follow the unpaved road 3.3 miles to a road split. Take the right fork 0.6 miles, descending to the campground and parking area at the end of the road.

Hiking directions: Walk 50 yards back up the entrance road to the signed Redwood Trail on the left by the yellow gate. Walk past the gate and down the road to a camping cabin. The signed footpath is on the right, just before reaching the cabin. Descend through the dense forest to a signed junction with the Tie Trail at 0.8 miles. Begin the loop on the right fork, staying on the Redwood Trail. Continue downhill, passing the old CCC bunkhouse on the left just before reaching a signed three-way junction at 1.7 miles. The right fork heads north on the Boundary Trail (Hike 33). Take the left fork on the Plum Trail, passing the old ranger station on the right. The narrow footpath gently leads a half mile uphill to a signed junction with the Tie Trail.

Leave the Plum Trail and bear left, ascending the mountain. At a half mile, complete the loop at the junction with the Redwood Trail. Take the right fork and return to the trailhead.

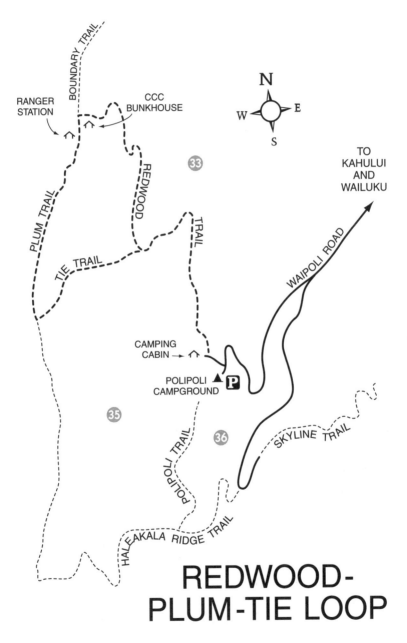

REDWOOD-PLUM-TIE LOOP

Hike 35
Polipoli Loop
Polipoli State Park

Hiking distance: 4.9 mile loop
Hiking time: 2.5 hours
Elevation gain: 1,000 feet
Maps: U.S.G.S. Lualailua Hills and Makena
   Recreation Trails of the Kula Forest Reserve

Summary of hike: The Polipoli Loop is a combination of four forested trails. The hike begins at the picnic area and campground on the Polipoli Trail and connects with the Haleakala Ridge Trail. A side path near the junction with the Plum Trail leads to a cinder cone containing a small shelter cave. The Plum Trail gently winds through redwood, ash and sugi pine groves, usually shrouded in an atmospheric mist. On the return leg of the loop is an old ranger station by a huge wall of flowering hydrangea bushes.

Driving directions: Follow the driving directions on page 68 to Waipoli Road. From Waipoli Road, continue 5.9 miles up this steep winding road to the end of the pavement. Follow the unpaved road 3.3 miles to a road split. Take the right fork 0.6 miles, descending to the campground and parking area at the end of the road.

Hiking directions: Facing the campground, take the signed Polipoli Trail on the right. Head south in the cedar, cypress and pine forest to a T-junction with the Haleakala Ridge Trail at 0.6 miles. Take the right fork, winding downhill through eucalyptus, mahogany and cypress around the west side of Polipoli Peak. At the junction, bear left for a short detour to the cinder cone and cave. Return to the junction and continue downhill to the end of the trail at 1.5 miles. Take the Plum Trail to the right (north) on a gentle grade along the contours of the mountainside. At 2.6 miles is a signed junction. The Tie Trail on the right returns back to Polipoli Park for a four-mile loop. Stay to the left, descending to the ranger station and the Redwood Trail junction 0.6 miles ahead. Begin ascending the mountain. Pass the CCC bunkhouse on the right and the Tie Trail junction, reaching a camping cabin near the campground. Bear left on the dirt road to the campground access road, and head back to the campground.

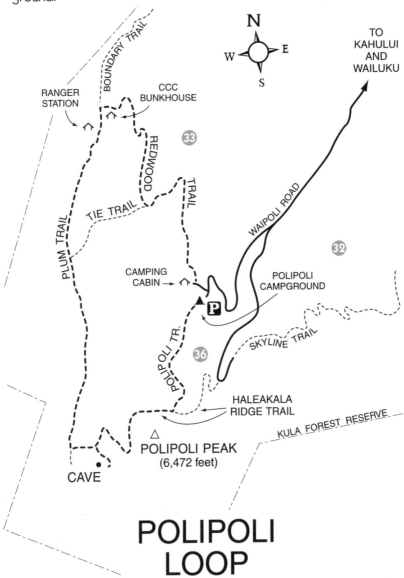

POLIPOLI LOOP

Hike 36
Polipoli-Haleakala Ridge Loop
Polipoli State Park

Hiking distance: 2.2 mile loop
Hiking time: 2 hours
Elevation gain: 400 feet
Maps: U.S.G.S. Lualailua Hills and Makena
Recreation Trails of the Kula Forest Reserve

Summary of hike: The Polipoli Trail begins at the campground and winds through lush old growth stands of cedar, alder, cypress and pine. The trail connects with the Haleakala Ridge Trail which follows the crest of Haleakala to spectacular vistas of Maui. The path ends at the Skyline Trail at 6,550 feet on a wide, flat overlook.

Driving directions: Follow the driving directions on page 68 to Waipoli Road. From Waipoli Road, continue 5.9 miles up this steep winding road to the end of the pavement. Follow the unpaved road 3.3 miles to a road split. Take the right fork 0.6 miles, descending to the campground and parking area at the end of the road.

Hiking directions: Facing the campground, take the signed Polipoli Trail on the right. Head south in the pine, cypress and cedar forest to a T-junction with the Haleakala Ridge Trail at 0.6 miles. The right fork leads to the cave and Plum Trail (Hike 35). Take the left fork on the Haleakala Ridge Trail, leaving the shade of the forest. Climb up the ridge to a grassy flat and overlook by the Skyline Trail switchback, a hairpin bend in the unpaved road. The right fork leads up the Skyline Road on a crest towards Haleakala. Take the left fork, heading downhill on the Waipoli Road. Descend 0.7 miles to the road split with the campground road. Bear sharply to the left, heading downhill through a eucalyptus forest and back to the campground 0.6 miles ahead.

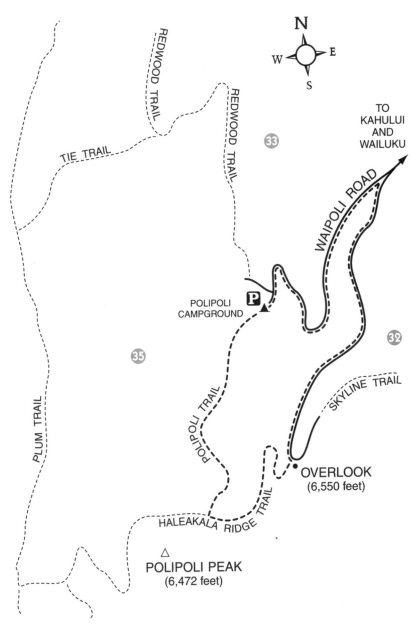

POLIPOLI-HALEAKALA
RIDGE LOOP

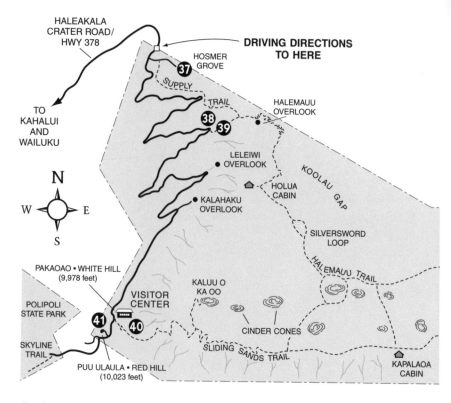

DRIVING DIRECTIONS
TO HERE

Haleakala is the world's largest dormant volcano. Its expansive crater stretches seven miles long, 2.5 miles wide and 3,000 feet deep. Twenty-seven thousand acres were designated as a Haleakala National Park to preserve its unique features. The twisting park road follows along the crater's west rim, the highest elevation on Maui. From the crater, the park extends east down the Kipahulu Valley to the ocean at Oheo Gulch south of Hana. A string of multi-colored cinder cones, lava flows and fields of volcanic ash line the surreal crater floor with 36 miles of interconnected, well-marked trails. Hikes 37 through 41 explore some of these trails, from the volcanic foothills to the 10,023-foot summit, and from the magnificent crater rim to the stark, lunar landscape of the crater floor. The trails lead to cinder cones, lava caves, panoramic overlooks and a camping cabin. Be sure to pack warm clothes, as the temperatures are much cooler at this 10,000-foot elevation.

HALEAKALA CRATER
HIKES 37–41

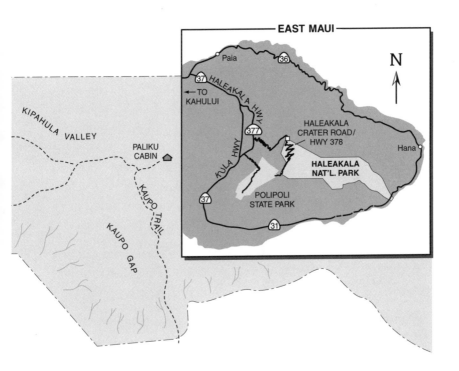

EAST MAUI

Paia 36

N

37 HALEAKALA HWY

←TO KAHULUI

377

KAHULU HWY

HALEAKALA CRATER ROAD/ HWY 378

KIPAHULA VALLEY

PALIKU CABIN

KAUPO TRAIL

37

POLIPOLI STATE PARK

HALEAKALA NAT'L. PARK

Hana

31

KAUPO GAP

Driving directions to Haleakala park boundary: From the junction of the Haleakala Highway (37) and the Hana Highway (36) near the airport, take the Haleakala Highway (37) upcountry. Head southeast 7.7 miles, a half mile past Pukalani, to the first junction with Highway 377. Turn left on Highway 377 (the Haleakala Highway), continuing uphill to a junction with Highway 378/Haleakala Crater Road. Turn left and zigzag up the mountain to the Haleakala park boundary.

Continue from the park boundary in accordance with each hike's directions.

Hike 37
Hosmer Grove
Haleakala National Park

Hiking distance: 0.7 mile loop
Hiking time: 30 minutes
Elevation gain: 100 feet
Maps: U.S.G.S. Kilohana
　　　　Trails Illustrated Haleakala National Park

Summary of hike: Hosmer Grove is an exotic botanical grove at 6,800 feet. It is 3,500 feet below the summit of Haleakala. In 1910, Ralph Hosmer, Hawaii's first territorial forester, planted this grove with introduced trees from around the world. He planted spruce, juniper and fir from the United States mainland, cedar and sugi pine from Japan, and eucalypti from Australia. The self-guided nature trail is an easy meandering stroll through the alien forest and continues through a native forest. The grove includes a picnic area and campground.

Driving directions: From the Haleakala park boundary, continue 0.1 mile to the signed Hosmer Grove Campground turnoff. Turn left and park in the parking lot by the trailhead.

Hiking directions: The signed trailhead is at the north end of the parking area adjacent to the campground. Take the well-marked trail past an interpretive sign, and wind through the alien forest. Cross a footbridge over a stream, and continue to an overlook with a bench. The path then weaves through the native Hawaiian shrubland. Return to the south end of the parking area.

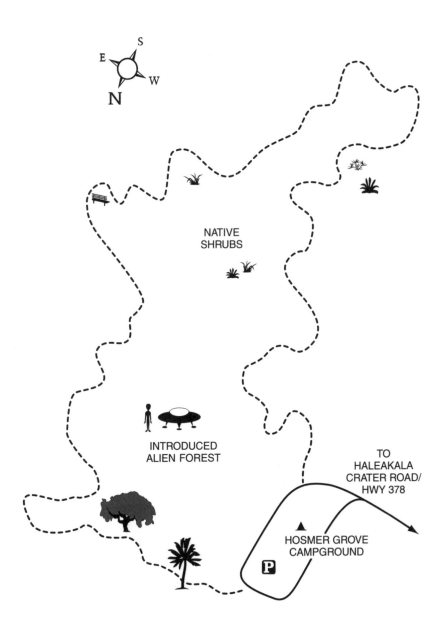

Compass directions (clockwise from top): S, W, N, E

NATIVE
SHRUBS

INTRODUCED
ALIEN FOREST

TO
HALEAKALA
CRATER ROAD/
HWY 378

HOSMER GROVE
CAMPGROUND

P

HOSMER GROVE

Hike 38
Halemauu Trail to Crater Rim Overlook
Haleakala National Park

Hiking distance: 1.5 miles round trip
Hiking time: 45 minutes
Elevation gain: 250 feet
Maps: U.S.G.S. Kilohana
　　　　 Trails Illustrated Haleakala National Park

Summary of hike: The Halemauu Trail descends from the west rim of the Haleakala Crater and crosses the crater floor to the eastern end. This hike follows the first mile of the trail, traversing the upper slope across the alpine scrubland to an overlook at the edge of the crater. From the rim are expansive views of the northern flanks of Haleakala, Koolau Gap and the moist cliffs of Leleiwi. The crater floor is dotted with several multi-colored cinder cones.

Driving directions: From the Haleakala park boundary, continue 4.5 miles to the trailhead turnoff on a sharp hairpin bend in the road, between mile markers 14 and 15. Turn left into the trailhead parking lot.

Hiking directions: Head southeast past the information sign and curve left towards the rim. Gradually descend along the slopes of Haleakala across the alpine shrubland. At 0.6 miles, pass the junction with the Supply Trail, a pack route from Hosmer Grove that intersects from the left. Continue down the easy descent on the rocky path to a trail gate. Pass through the gate and zigzag down a short distance to the rim of the crater and overlook. This is our turnaround spot.

To hike further, continue with Hike 39. The switchbacks steeply descend over 1,000 feet along the crater wall. Follow the crater floor, reaching Holua Cabin at 3.9 miles from the trailhead.

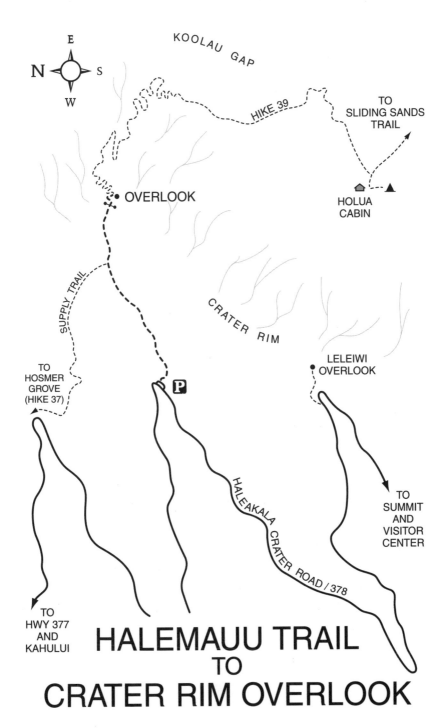

KOOLAU GAP

N E S W

HIKE 39

TO SLIDING SANDS TRAIL

HOLUA CABIN

OVERLOOK

SUPPLY TRAIL

CRATER RIM

TO HOSMER GROVE (HIKE 37)

LELEIWI OVERLOOK

P

HALEAKALA CRATER ROAD / 378

TO SUMMIT AND VISITOR CENTER

TO HWY 377 AND KAHULUI

HALEMAUU TRAIL
TO
CRATER RIM OVERLOOK

Hike 39
Halemauu Trail to Holua Cabin
Haleakala National Park

Hiking distance: 7.8 miles round trip
Hiking time: 4 hour
Elevation gain: 1,400 feet
Maps: U.S.G.S. Kilohana
Trails Illustrated Haleakala National Park

Summary of hike: The Halemauu Trail to Holua Cabin descends the sheer cliffs of Haleakala on the west crater wall. The trail begins at 8,000 feet, where dramatic switchbacks zigzag down to Koolau Gap on the crater floor. Along the way are magnificent views into the crater and down the Keanae Valley to the ocean. On the cliffs behind the cabin is a cave; a hundred yards to the east is a lava tube. This hike can be combined with the Sliding Sands Trail (Hike 40) for a one-way 11.5-mile shuttle hike.

Driving directions: From the Haleakala park boundary, continue 4.5 miles to the trailhead turnoff on a sharp hairpin bend in the road, between mile markers 14 and 15. Turn left into the trailhead parking lot.

Hiking directions: Follow the hiking directions from Hike 38 to the overlook at the rim of the crater. From the overlook, begin the awesome descent, snaking down the narrow ridge on steep switchbacks. The moonscape views inside the crater are magnificent. At the crater floor by Koolau Gap is a trail gate. Pass through the gate and follow the floor along the base of the crater wall through a grassy meadow. At 3.9 miles, the trail reaches a signed junction by Holua Cabin, sitting above the trail on a lava plateau. This is our turnaround spot. The right fork leads to the cabin on a grassy flat near the crater wall. A short distance to the south of the cabin is a campground.

From the junction, the Halemauu Trail continues to a junction with the Sliding Sands Trail and on to the east end of the crater.

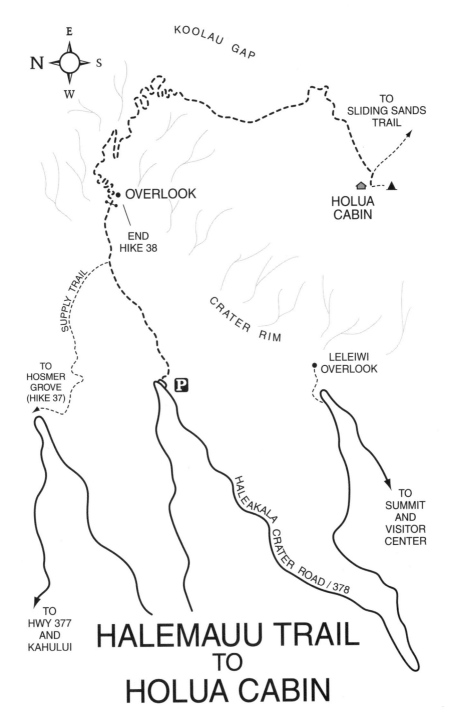

KOOLAU GAP

N E S W

TO SLIDING SANDS TRAIL

OVERLOOK

HOLUA CABIN

END HIKE 38

SUPPLY TRAIL

CRATER RIM

TO HOSMER GROVE (HIKE 37)

P

LELEIWI OVERLOOK

TO SUMMIT AND VISITOR CENTER

HALEAKALA CRATER ROAD / 378

TO HWY 377 AND KAHULUI

HALEMAUU TRAIL
TO
HOLUA CABIN

Hike 40
Sliding Sands Trail to Kaluu o Ka Oo
Haleakala National Park

Hiking distance: 5 miles round trip
Hiking time: 3 hours
Elevation gain: 1,600 feet
Maps: U.S.G.S. Kilohana
      Trails Illustrated Haleakala National Park

Summary of hike: Kaluu o Ka Oo is a multi-colored cinder cone on the south end of the Haleakala Crater. The cinder cone is below the ridge of Red Hill near the summit of Haleakala. The Sliding Sands Trail, located by the visitor center, descends into the crater on a cinder and ash path. The trail follows the base of the south rim into the barren moonscape with continuous magnificent vistas. A half-mile spur trail climbs to the rim of Kaluu o Ka Oo, offering views into the cinder cone.

Driving directions: From the Haleakala park boundary, continue 10.5 miles to the visitor center parking lot on the left, near the summit of Haleakala.

Hiking directions: Circle around to the right (south) side of Pakaoao (White Hill), and parallel the road for a short distance to the rim of the crater. You will see Kaluu o Ka Oo (the first cinder cone below), and the Sliding Sands Trail disappearing into the stark vastness. Begin the steady descent on a few switchbacks into the immense crater along the south wall. At just under a mile, pass a distinct rock formation with flowering shrubs. Curve right, away from the outcropping. Continue down to a signed junction at two miles by lava formations near the crater floor. Leave the Sliding Sands Trail and bear left (north). Descend steeply, then the path levels out and traverses the hillside towards the cinder cone. Pass numerous silversword plants and begin the short ascent to the edge of the colorful cone. Look into the depression from atop Kaluu o Ka Oo. A rough trail circles the rim.

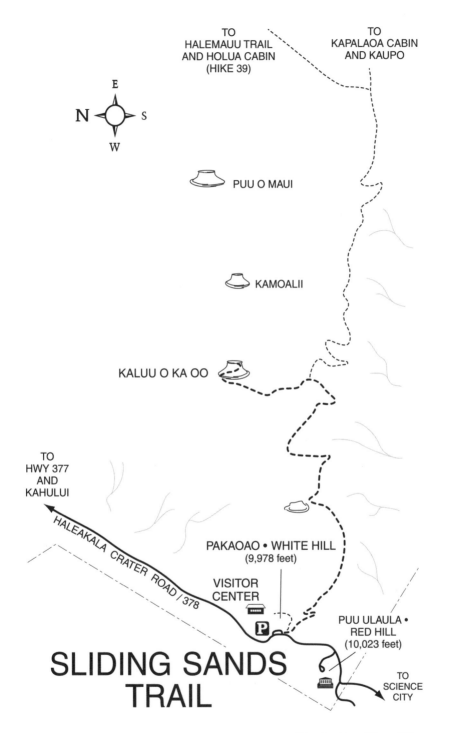

TO
HALEMAUU TRAIL
AND HOLUA CABIN
(HIKE 39)

TO
KAPALAOA CABIN
AND KAUPO

N E S W

PUU O MAUI

KAMOALII

KALUU O KA OO

TO
HWY 377
AND
KAHULUI

HALEAKALA CRATER ROAD / 378

PAKAOAO • WHITE HILL
(9,978 feet)

VISITOR
CENTER

P

PUU ULAULA •
RED HILL
(10,023 feet)

TO
SCIENCE
CITY

SLIDING SANDS
TRAIL

Hike 41
Pakaoao (White Hill) and Puu Ulaula (Red Hill)
Haleakala National Park

Hiking distance: 0.7 miles round trip
Hiking time: 1 hour
Elevation gain: 150 feet
Maps: U.S.G.S. Kilohana
Trails Illustrated Haleakala National Park

Summary of hike: Pakaoao (White Hill) is the favorite spot for experiencing the world-renowned Haleakala sunrise. White Hill is adjacent to the visitor center, with a book store and exhibits about the volcano. The awesome views from the 9,778 hilltop extend into and across the immense crater.

Puu Ulaula (Red Hill) is a cinder cone on the southwest rim of Haleakala. At 10,023 feet, the hill is the highest spot on Maui. The vistas take in the entire island of Maui, the offshore islands of Lanai, Molokai and Kahoolawe and the Big Island to the southeast. A 360-degree glass-enclosed observation and exhibit building allows for weather-sheltered panoramic views.

Driving directions: From the Haleakala park boundary, continue 10.5 miles to the visitor center parking lot on the left near the summit of Haleakala.

Puu Ulaula Overlook is 0.5 miles past the visitor center at the enclosed observation shelter on Maui's highest point. Park in the lot by the shelter.

Hiking directions: The White Hill hike begins at the visitor center. The short quarter-mile trail loops to the right (south). Curve around the basaltic knob on the gentle grade, gaining 150 feet up to the summit. The path nearly forms a loop. From the overlook, Sliding Sands Trail (Hike 40) can be seen disappearing into the vast crater.

The Red Hill stroll circles the parking area from the summit of Maui. The paths take you to numerous vista overlooks and the glass-enclosed viewing shelter. Meander along your own route.

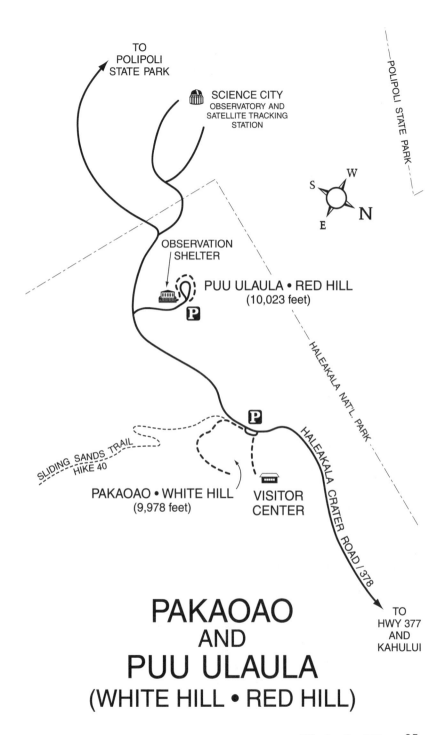

TO
POLIPOLI
STATE PARK

SCIENCE CITY
OBSERVATORY AND
SATELLITE TRACKING
STATION

POLIPOLI STATE PARK

W
S
N
E

OBSERVATION
SHELTER

PUU ULAULA • RED HILL
(10,023 feet)

P

HALEAKALA NAT'L. PARK

P

SLIDING SANDS TRAIL
HIKE 40

PAKAOAO • WHITE HILL
(9,978 feet)

VISITOR
CENTER

HALEAKALA CRATER ROAD / 378

TO
HWY 377
AND
KAHULUI

PAKAOAO
AND
PUU ULAULA
(WHITE HILL • RED HILL)

Hike 42
Waihou Spring Trail

Hiking distance: 2.4 miles round trip
Hiking time: 1.5 hours
Elevation gain: 400 feet
Maps: U.S.G.S. Kilohana
        Maui Recreation Map

Summary of hike: Waihou Spring Trail is above the up-country town of Makawao in the Waihou Spring Forest Reserve. The beautiful reserve borders the state-run tree experimentation project planted in the 1920s. The trail begins on the tree plantation road and loops through a forest of Monterey cypress, pines, eucalypti and koa. A side path leads to an overlook and descends into Kailua Gulch at an enclosed, boulder-strewn canyon with numerous caves. Old water diversion tunnels are cut into the face of the surrounding cliffs.

Driving directions: From Hana Highway (36) in downtown Paia, take Baldwin Avenue 7 miles upcountry to Makawao Avenue in the town of Makawao. Continue straight through the intersection—Baldwin Avenue changes to Olinda Road. Drive 4.9 miles up the winding road to the Waihou Spring trailhead on the right by the signed Tree Growth Research Area entrance, located 0.9 miles past mile marker 11.

Hiking directions: Walk past the signed gate, and take the unpaved road south into the pine forest. The soft trail, covered in pine needles, borders the tree experimentation project on the left. At 0.2 miles, as the road curves left, leave the road and take the signed trail to the right. Continue under the shade of a dense forest canopy to a junction at 0.4 miles. Begin the loop to the right to a signed junction with the spur trail to the over-look and spring. Bear right on the narrow footpath, and head gently downhill a quarter-mile to an overlook with a bench. Switchbacks lead down the hillside to the rock-enclosed forested canyon. Numerous caves are in the surrounding cliffs.

The spring is dry but the location is fascinating to explore. Return up the mountain past the overlook and back to the loop trail. Go to the right, meandering through the open forest and completing the loop. Return to the right.

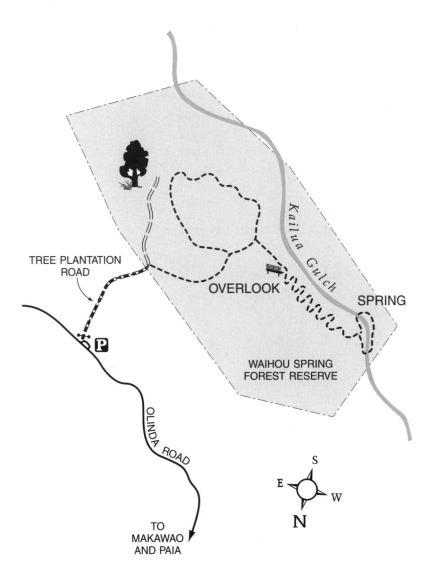

WAIHOU SPRING

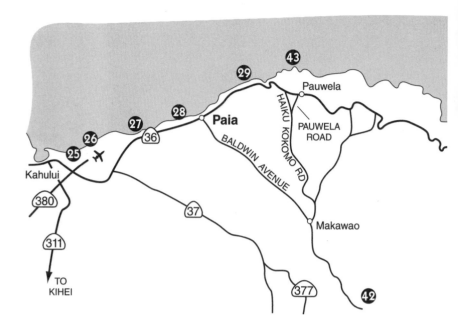

THE HANA HIGHWAY
HIKES 43–55

The Hana Highway is a gorgeous, winding 55-mile road that traverses the northeast slopes of Haleakala along the edge of the windward coastal cliffs. Along the way are magnificent waterfalls, freshwater swimming pools, diverse beaches, moist lowland forests, lush rainforests, deep stream-fed canyons, steep valleys, breathtaking seascape vistas, state and county parks, and more than fifty one-lane bridges. This is among the most scenic drives in Hawaii and the world. The drive is a slow trek with many magnificent places to stop, hike, swim and explore, easily making the trip a full day's experience. It is advisable not to rush by spending a night or two in Hana.

Hikes 43 through 49 are on the road to Hana, and Hikes 50 through 55 are in the town of Hana or a short distance beyond. From Paia, Hana is 44 miles—driving directions and mileages originate from Paia.

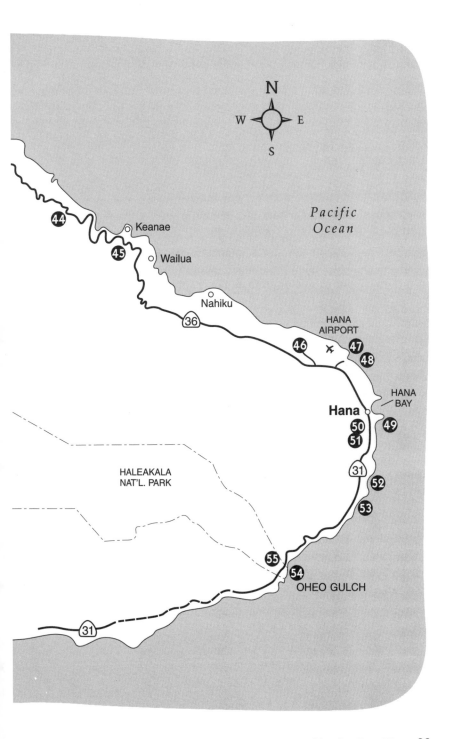

Hike 43
Pauwela Point and Lighthouse

Hiking distance: 1 mile round trip
Hiking time: 40 minutes
Elevation gain: Level
Maps: U.S.G.S. Haiku
       Island of Maui Recreation Map

Summary of hike: Pauwela Point and the lighthouse (basically a light on a pole) sit on beautiful sea cliffs on the west edge of Kuiaha Bay. The trail follows the edge of the flat, grassy bluffs overlooking the coconut palm-lined bay with great coastal views from more than 100 feet above the ocean. The stream-fed bay is surrounded by private property and has no public access.

Driving directions: From the junction of the Hana Highway (36) and Baldwin Avenue in downtown Paia, take the Hana Highway 5.2 miles to the turnoff on the left, 0.1 mile past the signed Pauwela Road turnoff. (It is across from the Haiku Maui Community Center.) Turn left and follow the unpaved cane road 1.2 miles to the lighthouse on the right. Park on the grassy flat near the cliffs.

Hiking directions: To the left, a steep and eroded path descends to a beach cove with tidepools—careful footing is a must. To the right, the path follows the edge of the bluffs overlooking Kuiaha Bay with its jagged rock formations and pools. The path curves along the cliffs to the southwest corner of the bay. At this point, access to the bay ends at a private property fenceline. Return along the edge of the cliffs or across the grassy parkland expanse.

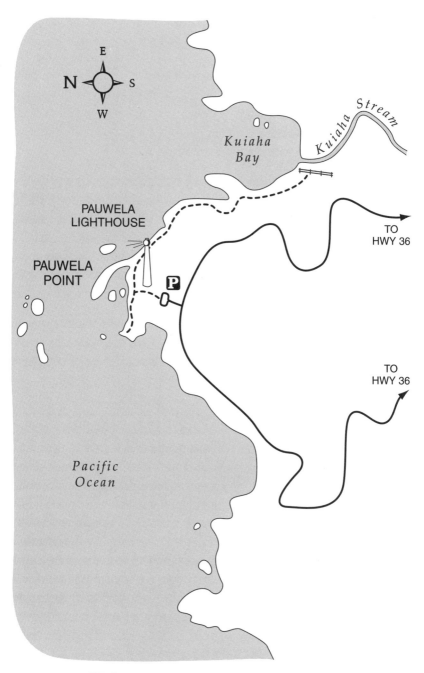

PAUWELA POINT

Hike 44
Waikamoi Ridge Trail

Hiking distance: 1.2 miles round trip
Hiking time: 30 minutes
Elevation gain: 200 feet
Maps: U.S.G.S. Keanae
      Island of Maui Recreation Map

Summary of hike: The Waikamoi Ridge Trail is an interpretive nature trail in a tropical forest. The trail climbs the dense vegetated slope to a grassy clearing and sheltered picnic area, offering great views of Keanae Peninsula and the ocean. A mosaic of tree roots crosses the trail through the lush rain forest that is adorned with groves of bamboo, paperback eucalypti, mahogany, heliconia, philodendrons and ginger.

Driving directions: From the junction of Hana Highway (36) and Baldwin Avenue in downtown Paia, take the Hana Highway 19.2 miles to the signed trailhead parking area on the right, between mile markers 9 and 10.

Hiking directions: Walk up the paved ramp past the trail sign to the first picnic area in a stand of large eucalypti. Take the path to the left, and descend through the lush forest for a short distance. Climb up the hillside to a bench at an overlook of a deep gorge, Waikamoi Stream and the Hana Highway. Continue up the steps, following the ridge to a junction. The right fork returns to the trailhead. Take the left fork uphill to a second trail split. Curve left and continue following the ridge. At a half mile the path ends on a grassy hilltop clearing at a sheltered picnic area and bamboo forest. Return on the same path back to the trail split. Take the route that is now on your left, heading downhill to the picnic area near the trailhead. Bear left, curving down to the parking area.

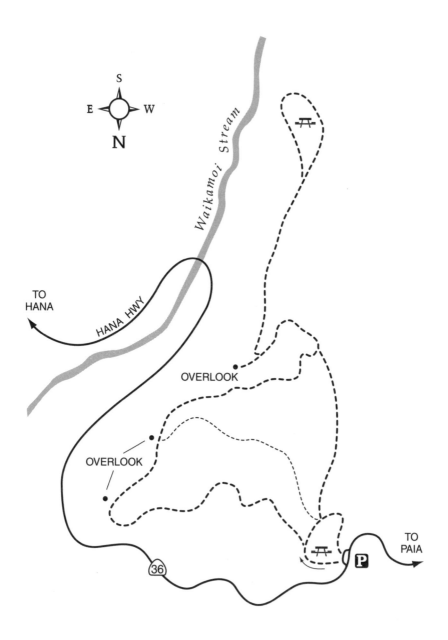

WAIKAMOI
RIDGE TRAIL

Hike 45
Keanae Arboretum

Hiking distance: 1.6 miles round trip
Hiking time: 1 hour
Elevation gain: Level
Maps: U.S.G.S. Keanae
      Island of Maui Recreation Map

Summary of hike: The Keanae Arboretum is a six-acre oasis with a profusion of flowering and fruit-bearing plants. The arboretum is divided into three sections—native forest trees, introduced tropical trees and cultivated Hawaiian plants. Piinaau Stream cascades from the rainforest through the lush arboretum, forming several swimming holes.

Driving directions: From the junction of Hana Highway (36) and Baldwin Avenue in downtown Paia, take the Hana Highway 26.3 miles to the parking pullouts on the right by the signed arboretum gates. The pullouts are located in a shady hairpin turn between mile markers 16 and 17.

Hiking directions: Pass the green gate and follow the jeep road 0.2 miles along Piinaau Stream to the signed Keanae Arboretum entrance gate. Inside the arboretum, the paved path parallels Piinaau Stream through an open grassy area with introduced fruit and ornamental trees. Short side paths lead down to the stream and pools. Continue along the unpaved path lined with ti plants. Pass through the Hawaiian cultivated plant section with irrigated taro patches between lava rock walls. There are banana, sweet potato, sugar cane, ginger and papaya plants. The rocky path skirts the taro patches to the south arboretum boundary at a half mile.

    To hike further, the muddy path narrows and is usually slippery. Cross Pokakaekane Stream, leave the banks of Piinaau Stream, and follow Kuo Stream through the rain forest. The trail frequently crosses the stream, passing small pools. Choose your own turnaround spot.

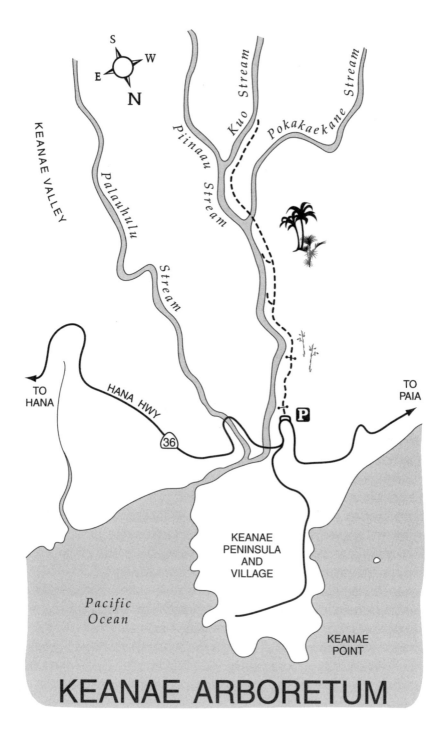

Hike 46
Ulaino Road Trail
to Blue Pool and Blue Angel Falls

Hiking distance: 4 miles round trip
Hiking time: 2 hours
Elevation gain: 120 feet
Maps: U.S.G.S. Hana
        Island of Maui Recreation Map

Summary of hike: Blue Angel Falls cascades 100 feet off the fern-covered lava cliffs into Blue Pool on the beach a few steps from the ocean. The hike down Ulaino Road passes through a lush tropical forest with kukui, hala and guava trees. The road ends at a cove by the abandoned village of Ulaino, where old stone walls overtaken by the jungle still remain. Heleleikeoha Stream flows through the rocky cove, forming a shallow lagoon before entering the sea.

Driving directions: From the junction of Hana Highway (36) and Baldwin Avenue in downtown Paia, take the Hana Highway 43.5 miles to the signed Ulaino Road. Turn left and drive 0.7 miles to the end of the paved road. Park alongside the road.

From Hana, drive 3 miles northwest on the Hana Highway to the Ulaino Road turnoff, located one mile past the signed Waianapanapa State Park turnoff.

Hiking directions: Follow the road northwest under the forest canopy. At a half mile, cross Honomaele Stream by Kahanu Gardens on the right. Continue through the forest, passing a few homesteads on each side of the road. Stay on the main road, disregarding smaller road forks. The trail ends near the mouth of Heleleikeoha Stream, where the stream empties into the ocean 100 yards to your right. Shortly before Heleleikeoha Stream, the remains of Ulaino village are on the right, which are gradually being overtaken by the jungle vegetation. Wade across the stream and follow the coastline west a few hundred yards along the cobblestone beach. Blue Angel

Falls and Blue Pool, a large swimming hole at the base of the waterfall, will be on the left. Return along the same path.

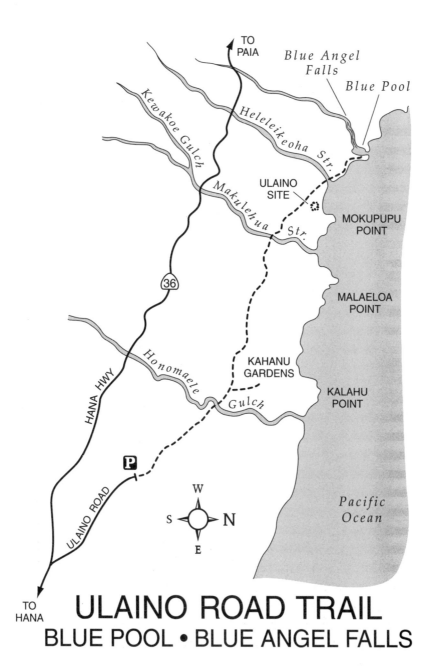

ULAINO ROAD TRAIL
BLUE POOL • BLUE ANGEL FALLS

Hike 47
Waianapanapa State Park to Pukaulua Point

Hiking distance: 2 miles round trip
Hiking time: 1 hour
Elevation gain: 50 feet
Maps: U.S.G.S. Hana
       Island of Maui Recreation Map

Summary of hike: The hike begins in Waianapanapa State Park (back cover photo) and follows a portion of the ancient Hawaiian "Kings Highway" from Pailoa Bay to Pakaulua Point. The path crosses Pailoa "Black Sand" Beach and parallels the volcanic coastline above the sea. Two small cobblestone beach pockets are revealed along the way.

Driving directions: From Hana, drive 2 miles northwest on the Hana Highway to the signed Waianapanapa State Park turnoff, just before mile marker 32. Turn right and drive a half mile down the forest road to the state park. Turn left and go 0.2 miles to the parking lot.
    From Baldwin Avenue in downtown Paia, take the Hana Highway 44.5 miles to the signed Waianapanapa State Park turnoff and turn left. Follow directions above.

Hiking directions: From the Black Sand Beach overlook, take the paved path to the right through a tree grove to a trail split. The right fork follows the bluffs on the cliffside trail towards Hana (Hike 48). Take the left fork, descending to the southeast end of the beach. Cross the sand to the cliffside path on the west end. Follow the path up the cliffs and descend into Pokohulu Cove and the cobblestone beach. Reclimb the hillside, following the coastline atop the cliffs to the north end of Pailoa Bay. Curve left into Keawaiki Bay, a small rock-lined cove. A side path descends into the water-worn pebble beach. The main trail weaves along the cliffs to the immense, exposed aa lava field. The loose lava rock makes for slower, unstable footing. At a half mile, the path reaches the Kapukaulua VABM monument at

Pukaulua Point. This is a good spot to sit and look over the surroundings before returning. Diehard hikers can continue across the expanse of loose and sharp lava, reaching the fenced Hana Airport at just over one mile.

If you wish to see the Waianapanapa Caves, head left from the parking lot. The paved trail leads to two freshwater caves in lush grottos covered with moss, ginger, ti and draping ferns.

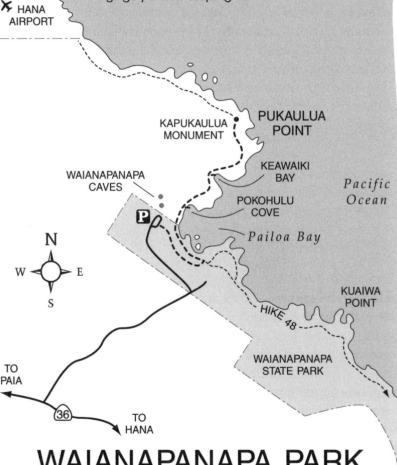

WAIANAPANAPA PARK
TO
PUKAULUA POINT

Hike 48
Hana-Waianapanapa Coastal Trail

Hiking distance: 4.5 miles round trip
Hiking time: 2.5 hours
Elevation gain: Nearly level
Maps: U.S.G.S. Hana
Island of Maui Recreation Map

Summary of hike: The Hana-Waianapanapa Trail follows a portion of the ancient "Kings Highway" from Pailoa Bay in Waianapanapa State Park (back cover photo) to Kainalimu Bay in a shady heliotrope grove northwest of Hana Bay. The hike follows the jagged, windswept coastal cliffs, crossing lava flows above caves, underground tunnels and irregular islets. The trail passes blowholes, sea arches, tidepools and an ancient Hawaiian temple site. Smooth hand-set stepping stones are still in place along the aa lava and cinder path.

Driving directions: Follow the driving directions from Hike 47 to the Waianapanapa State Park.

Hiking directions: Take the paved path to the right through a tree grove to a trail split. The left fork descends to Black Sand Beach (Hike 47). Follow the right fork across the basalt bluffs above Pailoa Bay to a second junction. The left fork follows the contours of the rugged coastline and rejoins the main trail a short distance ahead. Continue past jagged lava formations and arches jutting out to sea. Cross a natural bridge over a turbulent ocean inlet. At 0.8 miles the path reaches the lava rock walls of Ohala Heiau, a good turnaround spot for a shorter hike. To continue, follow the smooth stepping stones, crossing through an old battered fence and wooden doorway. A side path on the left leads to an overlook and cave. Cross the lava field on the edge of the towering cliffs to a fishermen's shelter at Luahaloa. Continue past Umalei Point on the rocky path. At 2.25 miles, the descending path reaches the rocky beach in Kainalimu Bay. Return along the same path or follow the shoreline to Hana Bay.

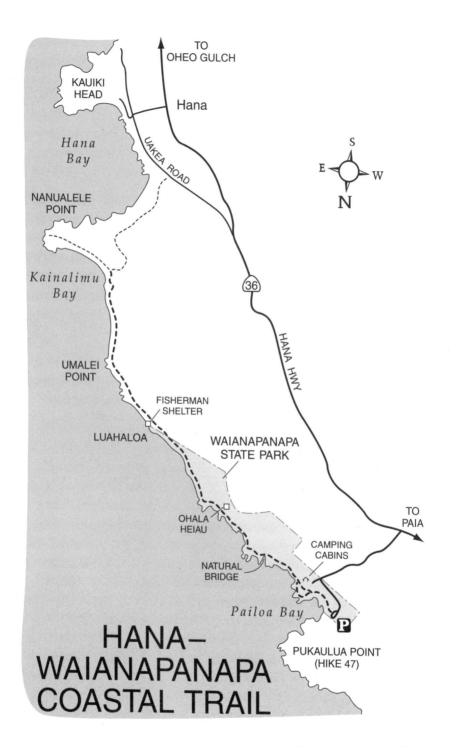

TO
OHEO GULCH

KAUIKI
HEAD

Hana

*Hana
Bay*

UAKEA ROAD

NANUALELE
POINT

36

*Kainalimu
Bay*

HANA HWY

UMALEI
POINT

FISHERMAN
SHELTER

LUAHALOA

WAIANAPANAPA
STATE PARK

TO
PAIA

OHALA
HEIAU

CAMPING
CABINS

NATURAL
BRIDGE

Pailoa Bay

P

HANA-
WAIANAPANAPA
COASTAL TRAIL

PUKAULUA POINT
(HIKE 47)

S
E   W
N

Hike 49
Kaihalulu "Red Sand" Beach

Hiking distance: 1 mile round trip
Hiking time: 1 hour
Elevation gain: 50 feet
Maps: U.S.G.S. Hana

Summary of hike: Kaihalulu "Red Sand" Beach is a hidden gem in the town of Hana on the isolated south side of Kauiki Head. The secluded, clothing-optional beach is set in a small pocket cove enclosed by towering volcanic cliffs. The red sand originates from the eroded volcanic cinders spilling off the cliffs. The exotic looking beach is often protected from the strong ocean currents by a large, jagged lava rock barrier that forms a natural sea wall. The only access to the beach is from a narrow, eroded cliff-hugging trail above the ocean.

Driving directions: From the town of Hana, take Uakea Road (by Hana Bay) 0.3 miles to the end of the road at the south end of Kauiki Head. Park along the side of the road.

Hiking directions: Facing the ocean, on the left side of the Hotel Hana Maui, cross the open field on the left towards Kauiki Head. Take the well-worn footpath, and curve towards the ocean to a trail split by a large ironwood tree. To the left is a Japanese cemetery. Take the right fork and descend on the short, steep path to the edge of the ocean cliffs. Bear left, below the cemetery, on the narrow path along the eroded cliffs. Use good judgement and caution as the footing is challenging due to loose cinders. A few dips and rises on the cliff shelf leads to the northeast point of Kaihalulu Bay. Curve around the point into the naturally carved amphitheater at Red Sand Beach. Descend the cliffs along the south end of the cove into the protected sandy beach pocket.

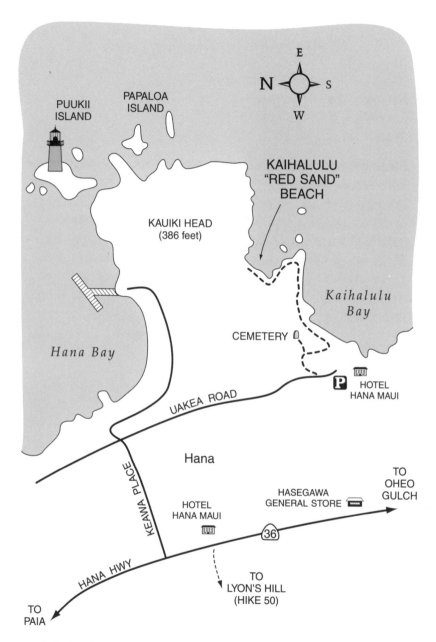

KAIHALULU "RED SAND" BEACH

Hike 50
Lyon's Hill to Fagan's Cross

Hiking distance: 1.5 miles round trip
Hiking time: 1 hour
Elevation gain: 500 feet
Maps: U.S.G.S. Hana

Summary of hike: Paul Fagan, founder of the Hotel Hana Maui in 1946 (Kauiki Inn), introduced cattle ranching to Hana. He purchased the cane-covered hills surrounding Hana and brought herds of Herefords from Molokai to establish Hana Ranch. Fagan's Cross, a memorial to Paul Fagan who passed away in 1960, sits atop the 545-foot summit of Puu O Kahaula, known as Lyon's Hill. This hike leads up to the lava rock cross. From the cross are incredible views overlooking the emerald green slopes across the town of Hana and Hana Bay. To the west (inland) are mountain views of Puu Hoolewa, Puu Kaukanu, Koaekea and Puu Puou.

Driving directions: The trail begins from the Hotel Hana Maui in the town of Hana along Highway 36. Park alongside the road by the hotel.

Hiking directions: The signed trailhead is across the street from the Hotel Hana Maui by the gazebo on the inland side of the road. Cross the grassy rolling pastureland on the paved path towards the prominent cross. Pass a junction with the Hana Maui Walking Trail on the left (Hike 51). Continue straight ahead towards the four tall palm trees. As you approach the base of Puu O Kahaula, curve to the right and traverse the north flank of the hill. At the ridge, continue past the cross to great views of the jagged ridge of the steep inland mountains. Loop around the back side of the hill, and head east for the final approach to Fagan's Cross. From the cross are views of the entire coastal area.

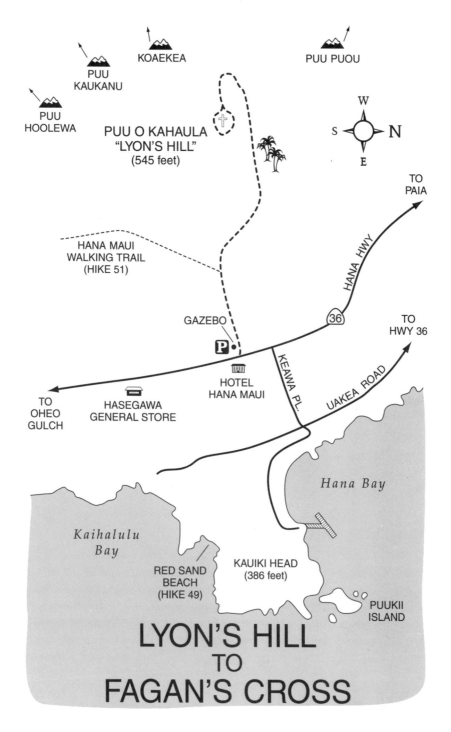

PUU
HOOLEWA

PUU
KAUKANU

KOAEKEA

PUU PUOU

W

S   N

E

PUU O KAHAULA
"LYON'S HILL"
(545 feet)

TO
PAIA

HANA MAUI
WALKING TRAIL
(HIKE 51)

HANA HWY

36

TO
HWY 36

GAZEBO

P

HOTEL
HANA MAUI

KEAWA PL.

UAKEA ROAD

TO
OHEO
GULCH

HASEGAWA
GENERAL STORE

Hana Bay

Kaihalulu
Bay

RED SAND
BEACH
(HIKE 49)

KAUIKI HEAD
(386 feet)

PUUKII
ISLAND

LYON'S HILL
TO
FAGAN'S CROSS

Hike 51
Hana Maui Walking Trail

Hiking distance: 3.5 miles round trip
Hiking time: 2 hours
Elevation gain: 150 feet
Maps: U.S.G.S. Hana
　　　　Hotel Hana Maui Area Map

Summary of hike: The Hana Maui Walking Trail crosses the Hana Ranch, an active cattle ranch. The trail across the emerald green slopes, dotted with grazing cattle, overlooks the town of Hana. The hike begins at the Hotel Hana Maui below Lyon's Hill and crosses the pastureland and two wooden bridges through forested groves.

Driving directions: The trail begins from the Hotel Hana Maui in the town of Hana along Highway 36. Park alongside the road by the hotel.

Hiking directions: The signed trailhead is across the street from the Hotel Hana Maui by the gazebo on the inland side of the road. Walk through the trail gate, past the gazebo and up the hill on the paved road. A short distance ahead is the signed trail on the left. The main trail, straight ahead, leads to Fagan's Cross on Lyon's Hill (Hike 50). Bear left on the footpath, crossing the rolling grasslands overlooking Kauiki Head, Hana Bay and the ocean. Pass the water tanks and cross a cattle guard. At 1.1 mile, the path enters a lush forest grove with papaya and guava trees. Cross two consecutive wooden bridges over Moomooiki Gulch and Moomoonui Stream at 1.3 miles. Views open up to Alau Island. At 1.75 miles, an electric cattle fence crosses the trail. To the left is Ka Iwi O Pele, the 440-foot red cinder hill on the coast by Koki Beach (Hike 52). This is a good turnaround spot.

To hike further, the trail continues across the fence, reaching Highway 31 at the junction with Haneoo Road. The road leads to Koki Beach and Hamoa Beach.

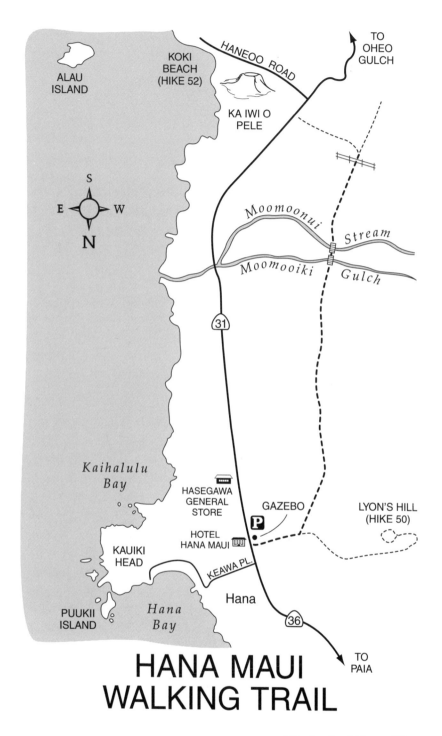

HANA MAUI
WALKING TRAIL

Hike 52
Koki Beach Park
and Hamoa Beach

Hiking distance: 0.6 miles round trip
Hiking time: 30 minutes
Elevation gain: Level
Maps: U.S.G.S. Hana

Summary of hike: Koki Beach Park is a roadside park south of Hana where the pastureland meets the sea. The tree-shaded beach sits at the southern edge of Ka Iwi o Pele, an eroded red cinder hill extending out to sea. A quarter mile off the coast is Alau Island, a seabird sanctuary with a 150-foot summit topped with coconut palms.

Driving directions: From the Hasegawa General Store in Hana, take the Hana Highway (36), which becomes Highway 31 at the edge of town, and drive south 1.5 miles to Haneoo Road between mile markers 50 and 51. Turn left and continue 0.4 miles to the oceanfront. Park on the left side of the road.

Hiking directions: Walk from the grassy park area to the shoreline. Follow the red and black sand beach left to the base of Ka Iwi o Pele, the 440-foot eroded cinder cone jutting into the ocean. At the north end of the beach, a grassy bluff leads up the edge of Ka Iwi o Pele to an overlook of the sea and Alau Island. The erosion of loose cinder on the volcanic hill makes going further dangerous. Return south and follow the walking path under the shade of the ironwood trees and naupaka bushes into Hokuula Bay, where the shoreline meets Haneoo Road.

A short distance further down Haneoo Road is Hamoa Beach, a beautiful palm-fringed pocket beach in a cove enclosed by cliffs. A lava rock wall lines the road. Steps lead down to the sandy shore at the head of Mokae Cove. The beach is owned by the Hotel Hana Maui but is open to the public.

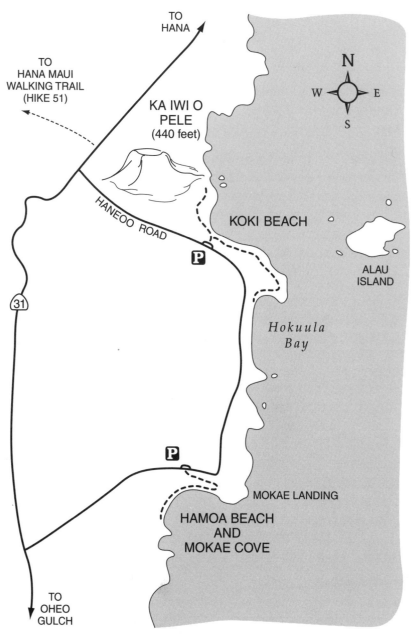

TO
HANA

TO
HANA MAUI
WALKING TRAIL
(HIKE 51)

KA IWI O
PELE
(440 feet)

HANEOO ROAD

KOKI BEACH

ALAU
ISLAND

P

31

Hokuula
Bay

P

MOKAE LANDING

HAMOA BEACH
AND
MOKAE COVE

TO
OHEO
GULCH

KOKI BEACH PARK
HAMOA BEACH

Hike 53
Venus Pool

Hiking distance: 0.6 miles round trip
Hiking time: 30 minutes
Elevation gain: 50 feet
Maps: U.S.G.S. Hana and Kipahulu

Summary of hike: Venus Pool is an undiscovered, little known gem between Hana and the Oheo Gulch Pools. The unmarked trail is quickly passed by the crowds heading south to the waterfalls and pools at Oheo Gulch. The trail crosses coastal pastureland to the ocean, where there are beautiful freshwater pools in the sculpted deep rock grottos.

Driving directions: From the Hasegawa General Store in Hana, take the Hana Highway (36), which becomes Highway 31 at the edge of town, and drive south 3.5 miles to a bridge just past mile marker 48. Park in the pullouts on the right after crossing the bridge.

Hiking directions: Walk back along the road and across the bridge over Waiohonu Stream. There is an opening in the gate on the ocean side of the road. Take the path east across the pastureland towards the ocean, parallel to Waiohonu Stream. Just before reaching the prominent, dome-shaped rock oven is a side path. Bear right on the path to two overlooks of the huge pools. The pools sit in a rock grotto with caves that about the ocean. Return to the main path by the rock oven, and continue along the edge of the bluffs overlooking the dynamic rock formations and pounding surf. Several side paths descend to the shoreline.

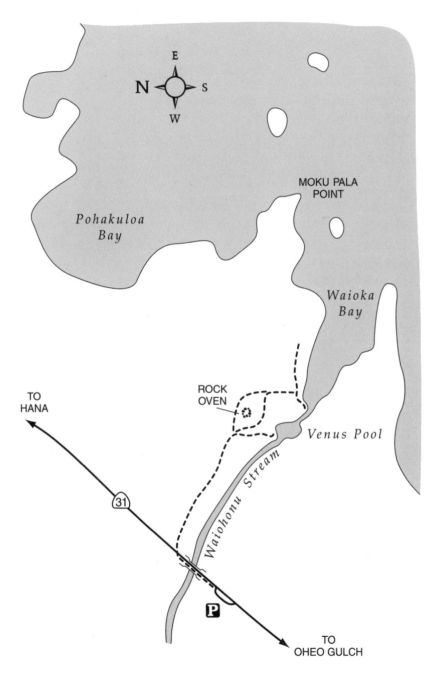

VENUS POOL

Hike 54
Seven Sacred Pools
Oheo Gulch

Hiking distance: 0.6 mile loop
Hiking time: 1 hour
Elevation gain: 100 feet
Maps: U.S.G.S. Kipahulu
           Trails Illustrated Haleakala National Park

Summary of hike: Oheo Gulch, commonly known as "Seven Sacred Pools," has a succession of natural staircase waterfalls cascading into a series of descending pools. The pools, numbering far more than seven, are bordered by sculpted lava rock basins and cliffs which lie along Oheo Gulch above the rugged eastern coastline at Kuloa Point. This short hike includes swimming holes and hikes around a series of freshwater pools that overlook the black lava rock oceanfront. Oheo Gulch is preserved as part of Haleakala National Park.

The twisting, winding road from Hana to the pools weaves along the coastline through valleys and ridges. The scenic drive passes waterfalls and crosses numerous one-lane bridges.

Driving directions: From Hana, drive 7 miles south on Highway 36, which becomes Highway 31 after Hana, to the signed parking lot past mile marker 42. It is on the ocean side of the road by the Kipahulu Ranger Station and visitor center.

Hiking directions: Follow the clearly marked path towards the visitor center and ocean. Cross the grassy slope and picnic area to the bluffs overlooking the ocean. On the right are rock wall remnants of an ancient Hawaiian village. Curve left, reaching the stream in Oheo Gulch by a series of five large swimming pools and numerous smaller pools, which are all connected by cascades and small waterfalls. Follow the succession of pools up the south side of Oheo Stream. At the bridge, a footpath returns to the parking lot.

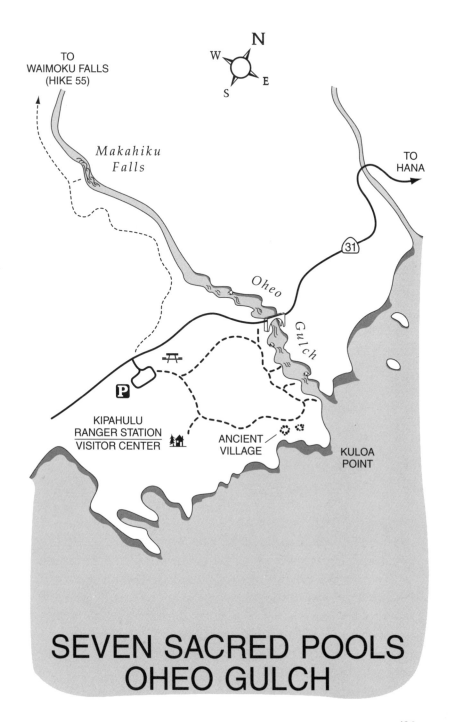

TO
WAIMOKU FALLS
(HIKE 55)

Makahiku Falls

N
W E
S

TO
HANA

31

Oheo Gulch

P

KIPAHULU
RANGER STATION
VISITOR CENTER

ANCIENT
VILLAGE

KULOA
POINT

SEVEN SACRED POOLS
OHEO GULCH

Hike 55
Pipiwai Trail to
Makahiku and Waimoku Falls

Hiking distance: 4 miles round trip
Hiking time: 2 hours
Elevation gain: 800 feet
Maps: U.S.G.S. Kipahulu
          Trails Illustrated Haleakala National Park

Summary of hike: Makahiku Falls and Waimoku Falls are towering cataracts on the streams above Oheo Gulch (Hike 54). Makahiku Falls, a half mile from the trailhead, plunges 185 feet off the forested cliff into the deep gorge. The trail ends further up the stream at the base of Waimoku Falls, set in a 400-foot rock wall amphitheater. The hike parallels Oheo Stream and Pipiwai Stream up the wet verdant valley, passing ancient taro farm sites and crossing two bridges. The jungle includes guava, mango, Christmas-berry trees and towering bamboo forests.

Driving directions: Follow the driving directions from Hike 54 to the Kipahulu Ranger Station and visitor center.

Hiking directions: The Pipiwai Trail begins on the inland side of the Hana Highway, across the road from the ranger station parking lot. Begin climbing up the pastureland along the left side of Oheo Gulch. At a half mile, a side path on the right leads to the forested Makahiku Falls cliffside overlook. Return to the main trail and continue uphill through the rain forest. At just under a mile, cross a bridge over Oheo Stream below the confluence of Palikea Stream and Pipiwai Stream, which form Oheo Stream. A short distance ahead, cross a second bridge over Pipiwai Stream. Enter the first of three cool and dark bamboo forests. Boardwalks aid in crossing the muddy areas. Just past the third bamboo forest, cross several channels of Pipiwai Stream to the shallow pool in front of Waimoku Falls. The waterfall free-falls off the moss and fern-covered cliffs into the pool. Return on the same path.

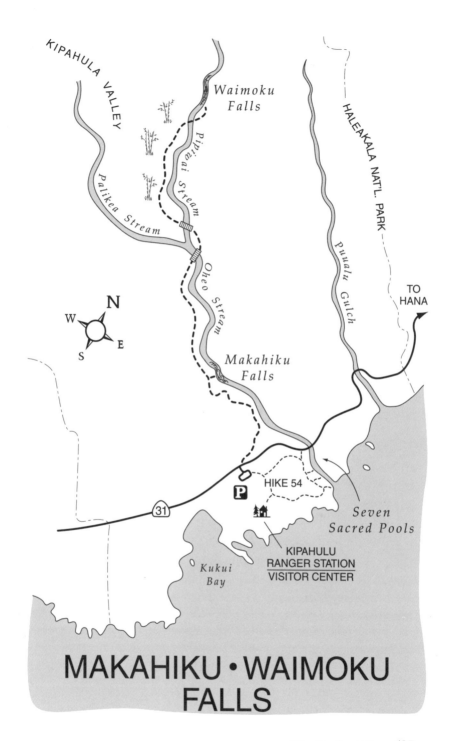

KIPAHULA VALLEY

Palikea Stream

Pipiwai Stream

Waimoku Falls

HALEAKALA NAT'L. PARK

Puualu Gulch

Oheo Stream

N
W   E
S

Makahiku Falls

TO HANA

HIKE 54

(31)

P

Seven Sacred Pools

KIPAHULU RANGER STATION
VISITOR CENTER

Kukui Bay

MAKAHIKU·WAIMOKU FALLS

Other Day Hike Guidebooks

These books may be purchased at your local bookstore or outdoor shop. Or, order them direct from the distributor:

The Globe Pequot Press
246 Goose Lane · P.O. Box 480 · Guilford, CT 06437-0480
www.globe-pequot.com

800-243-0495

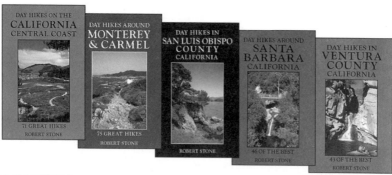

Notes